THRASHER
Skid Row Eskimo

Listen to the North Wind. It has come to take us away. The name, Inuvialuit, will only be heard in the wind. The land will still be there, the moon will still shine, the Northern Lights will still be bright, and the Midnight Sun will still be seen. But we will be gone forever . . .

Anthony Apakark Thrasher

Thrasher . . .
Skid Row Eskimo

by Anthony Apakark Thrasher
in collaboration with
Gerard Deagle and Alan Mettrick

GRIFFIN HOUSE
TORONTO 1976

ISBN 0 88760 082 4

Published by Griffin Press Limited,
461 King Street West, Toronto, M5V 1K7, Canada

Canadian Cataloguing in Publication Data

Thrasher, Anthony Apakark, 1937-
    Thrasher

ISBN 0-88760-082-4

1. Thrasher, Anthony Apakark, 1937-   2. Eskimos –
Northwest Territories - Mackenzie District. I. Deagle,
Gerard. II. Mettrick, Alan. III. Title.

E99.E7T47   970'.004'97   C76-017142-4

Printed and bound in Canada

Contents

Foreword

This book ends with the author, who is an Eskimo, on his way to a hospital for the criminally insane. It ends there because to wait for a happy ending is to wait for the musk-ox and the white fox to return to a white and simple north.

Anthony Apakark Thrasher has since been released from that institution but he is not better and the bad things go on happening. He has written an honest and true book and to hold out hope is to cheat on him.

Thrasher wrote most of the book in jail while awaiting trial on a murder charge. He wrote it in pencil on literally thousands of scraps of paper. Subsequently he was convicted of a lesser charge of manslaughter in the beating death of an old man called Charles Ratkovitch. He was sentenced to fifteen years. On appeal the prison term was reduced to seven years. During his time in prison he continued writing. Calgary lawyer William Stilwell, who acted for Thrasher in the case, encouraged him to write his story, and had the resulting material transcribed. If it had not been for him the story would not have come to print.

In the beginning Tony Thrasher was an Eskimo living on the Arctic Circle in the old way, a world apart from other Canadians. He was one of the youngest in a family of twenty-one children. He lived in a tent made of stretched caribou skins with ice windows, and ate only raw food. In the prime of his life he became a symbol of something new that was happening in the far north, a crutch for a niggardly white conscience. In the end none of it was that simple.

He was nineteen years old when a government man asked him if he wanted to go south and take a job training course. "The old days are gone. The days that your father knew are gone for ever," the man told him. And he was right, of course.

So the Canadian government flew Thrasher and a number of other young Eskimos from Tuktoyaktuk and Aklavik and Paulatuk, to Edmonton, Alberta. The first flush toilet any of them ever used was on that plane. In Edmonton they saw their first traffic lights and picked up jaywalking tickets in clumps before they learned to understand when they could cross the street and where. They had no idea how to use sidewalks, and a bunch of them would walk in formation, like mad soldiers, taking up the whole of the space so that there was no room for anyone else to pass. They bought Hudson's Bay suits and wore them over the pyjamas they had also bought for the first time.

Thrasher watched white men and tried to imitate their habits. So he slicked his hair down with Noxzema, brushed his teeth with shaving lather, and washed his face with mouthwash. He couldn't read labels and he chewed laxatives one after another, believing them to be candy.

Somewhere the baggage was lost so that the Eskimos arrived in Edmonton, to be billeted in a Skid Row hotel, with no money at all. Even before he had his first meal in a city restaurant, Thrasher was thrown in with bums and prostitutes and had got drunk and slept with a woman. While the Eskimos smiled for newspaper photographs, because they were told to smile, many of them were already deathly ill from the conditions and the heat they had been flown into.

Funny, tragic stories. Much of it is hard to believe, but if it is anything at all this story is true. As reporters, and as whites, we were sceptical often. So we checked. Right down to the name of an aircraft which is in Thrasher's script but not in Jane's *All the World's Aircraft*. De

Havilland said there had been such a plane, just one, and that it had operated where and when Thrasher had specified. His memory for incidents, names, dates and places is remarkable. So is his evocative, bitter style.

Thrasher's antecedents go far back into the haunting antiquity of Eskimo mythology. He is descended from medicine men. His own life has parallelled the process of urbanisation in the North. The year he was born, 1937, was the year the Anglican and Roman Catholic Missions were founded in Tuktoyaktuk. His father, Billy Thrasher, was helpmate to the first missionary Fathers.

Now, almost 40 years later the inquiry into the Mackenzie Valley Pipeline, headed by Mr. Justice Thomas Berger has become a forum on the future of the northland. Native people have told an unprecedented audience across the nation of their concerns. Yet their presentations of necessity had to be brief word-paintings of the blight they fear, the frustration they feel. The real meaning of it all is swallowed up in the end by some amnesia of the imagination.

Thrasher leaves very little to the imagination, least of all his own character blemishes.

Our role was to collate what was essentially a loose-leaf diary into narrative form, authenticate that narrative as thoroughly as possible and expand it.

Gerry Deagle
Alan Mettrick
June, 1976

x

Author's Preface

Alcohol has drugged the Eskimo. Today we are a shamed people. It killed my mother. It made my stepmother blind. It took me from a place where the game was never easy to hunt, where the cold was never easy to stand, but where I got a satisfaction out of life, to a country that's like a jungle to me.

In the North, polar bears hunt and share a meal. They even leave some for the foxes, and the foxes share what they have. I came down here and saw human beings preying on each other, pawing one another. On the Arctic coast, I could be completely lost and know what to do. But when I get lost in a city, I'm like a white man stranded on an iceberg with nothing but his clothes on.

I hope the younger generation of my people read my story. They will be easy targets, like me, if they are not warned. They should be told, not only about the good side of life in the South, but about the other part. The part that was hidden from me.

I never could tell who the good people are down here, the ones with homes. They are the people I could not reach. Their doors were always locked.

I still haven't seen the beautiful cities I saw in those pictures they gave me when I was a child . . . pictures of the outside world. Maybe I started at the wrong place or got thinking the wrong ideas.

There are 15,000 of us in the North. We need help if we are not to lose everything. We can't let the white man destroy everything we had before he came.

We have been silent too long.

Anthony Apakark Thrasher

Part One

You never went to Hell on Venials

1

Grade One Captive

In the twilight of the Arctic afternoon, the Roman Catholic nuns in their grey habits moved swiftly across the frozen ground of the mission property in Aklavik, as if driven by the North Wind itself.

I could see them darting towards me from the biggest of the four or five wooden buildings knotted together near the shore of Peel Harbour. The water was just beginning to get a thin coat of ice.

"Anthony...? Anthony!" they shouted.

Six years old, I stood trembling at the edge of the property, refusing to take one more step into that strange, forbidding world of mission school, my little bit of luggage slouched at my feet.

The nuns with their shrieking voices reminded me of the ghosts of the dead that my father said roamed the North in winter. It wasn't winter, it was fall. But I was scared just the same.

The dark shadowy forms closing around me struck terror in my heart. I didn't want to go to school. I wanted to be a trapper and hunter like my father, back home in Tuktoyaktuk, a hundred miles away on the Arctic Coast.

"Come here this instant, child!" they demanded. "We won't hurt you."

Breaking into tears, I turned and started to flee. But there was nowhere to run. Behind me was only the low bank leading down to the dock, where the two crewmen who had rowed me across the shallows were pushing off the tiny skiff. Behind that—nothing but the deep West Channel of the wide Mackenzie Delta where *The Immaculata*, the big schooner which had brought me from Tuk, was waiting to weigh anchor.

Suddenly there was a violent rustling behind me and I felt myself being lifted into the air. I let out a holler that could be heard clear around the North Pole. They had me by the hood of my Eskimo parka and I was dragged, kicking and screaming, into the big school house.

I was taken up some stairs into a small room with a big round tub where I was scrubbed so hard, and for so long, I thought I was going to turn white all over. They even checked my hair for bugs. Found some, too. And then they pushed me into a long room with beds filled with a lot of other little Eskimo boys, and some Indian and white children, and I slept in clean white sheets for the first time in my life.

That was nice. But I missed my father. Perhaps he didn't want to send me away but the priests at the Church had told him I needed an education, needed to learn of the ways of civilization down South, because soon the Eskimo people would no longer be able to live in the old way.

The next morning I was put in what they called the babies' class. I wasn't a real baby. I was almost old enough to trap fur, but they put me there anyway. Right from the start I had trouble learning, because I was always distracted by thoughts of my family and the things we used to do together . . .

The spring of 1940.

A good sunny day and a whole bunch of us fell through a wide-open crack in the ice close to Paulatuk. That's where we lived then. It's a tiny hunting village on

Darnley Bay off Amundsen Gulf on the Arctic Coast. I was almost three. My little sister, Agnes, was floating next to me, and a kettle and some cans were drifting around. My mother's legs were sticking out of the water. I could see little Johnny in her pack, bobbing up behind her. My dad, Bill, was splashing around nearby.

With the help of Johnny Rubens and some other neighbours, we got out. I could hear people laughing. Agnes and I were cold and stiff, as frozen as seal blubber. My mother wasn't so stiff, but she sure was mad. Dad was catching Holy Hell from her, as Agnes and I crawled under some stretched caribou skins to get warm. There were some bugs under there and I had the time of my life chewing them out. They were nice and round, white and juicy.

The Thrasher family was a whopping big one—twenty-one children. I was one of the youngest. Our home was a big tent set up next to the Catholic Mission House, which was the only wooden building in that quiet little place. Other Eskimo families lived in tents there, too. The tents were made from dozens of caribou skins, rigged up with the fur on the outside. In the freezing cold of winter, with the snow drifting over the barren plain, about all you could see from a distance, except for the Mission House, were the tiny wisps of smoke coming from the tin stacks sticking out of the roofs. Big ice windows let the light in when the long rays of the Arctic sun, for three or four hours each afternoon, cut through the eerie northern mist. At night, inside the tents, warm oil stoves kept us children snug and safe from the storms with their howling seventy-mile-an-hour winds that often came up without warning, chilling the air outside to a hundred degrees below zero.

In Paulatuk, there wasn't much for little children to do except run around and get into mischief.

Early in the morning the men would go off with their

dog teams to tend the traplines and we would stay behind
with the women and the old people—playing games with
the puppies until sleep caught them, and then we would
sleep, too. Later, we would gather around the old men to
watch them carve tools and little scenes from their own
hunting days. As they carved, they would tell us stories
about the great hunts along the Arctic Coast in days gone
by, about the great catches they had made in their
younger years. Towards late afternoon, the old men
would tell us to go and sit at the edge of the village and
watch for the trappers. We would see them before long,
just tiny specks on the horizon at first, coming across the
low Paulatuk Hills with their dogs. And then we would
hear shouting, getting louder, and our own excitement
would rise too. As the men neared the village, we would
run out to meet them, looking wide-eyed at the loads on
their sleds. We would watch as the catches were skinned,
to be stretched by the women over the long, wooden racks
to dry.

Those missionary Fathers. Some of them could really
take a joke. I remember Midnight Mass that year. It was
in full swing and I was seated beside our adopted brother,
Simon Koblu, who always fell asleep in church. Simon
was Eddie's boy. When Old Eddie died, my dad took
Simon home with him and he became one of us. He was
quite a character, twenty-one years old with the mentality
of a child. To me, he seemed quite normal, but at times
people were afraid of him. I wasn't. He hated liquor. He
hated women. He loved candies, singing, work and playing. He was never sick, and he would cry when he got
scolded.

Simon was nodding away beside me. My brother,
Tommy, who was a year older than me, was sitting on his
other side. There were no backs on the benches, and suddenly Simon went over backwards, taking Tommy and
me down with him. I was howling on the floor, and Fa-

ther Biname was laughing fit to bust, along with the whole congregation. We finished whatever was left of the Mass with a giggle.

After Mass, Father Biname passed out some big chocolate bars and candies, along with some balloons. I had trouble with the balloons, because I ate them, too. I was glad to get back home to the tent to get some frozen meat into my stomach, to chase them down.

Father Biname used to preach to us in Eskimo. But along came a new priest, big and tough, and he preached of fire and brimstone like a Holy Roller. His name was Father Griffimle and he used to scare the daylights out of us, shaking his finger and hollering. I hid under a bench most of the time. I would pity the poor devils from Hell if Father Griffimle ever got hold of them. I don't think there was an evil spirit within fifty miles of Paulatuk.

There were a lot of trappers, though. Wallace Brown was one. He stayed on a stretch of land at Cape Parry, which is straight north along the shore of Darnley Bay. Wallace lived mostly on seal meat and white foxes. I remember him most for his toughness, an old man of seventy, walking from Cape Parry to Paulatuk with his two dogs. He would come out of nowhere when we least expected to see him, wearing sealskin boots, with worn-out knees patched up with canvas and the fur half gone on his caribou-skin parka. One thing he always wore was a big smile.

Jim Fiji was another good trapper friend. He just disappeared one spring. His tracks left his house and went out to the edge of the bay. I guess the ice drifted out, carrying him along. There was a search by the village families, and the Royal Canadian Mounted Police came with their husky dogs and did an investigation, but with no results. Nobody knows exactly what happened to him. But there was talk among the old people that he probably was crushed by the dangerous moving sea ice out in the gulf. If you're caught by a crushing, rolling ice ridge, there isn't much hope of getting out alive.

Sometime early in '41, when I was four, my mother died. I was too small to understand. After that I thought my sister, Mary, was my mother, and I used to cry for Mary's milk. She took care of me until she went away to marry a man called Edgar. Then my little sister Agnes became my constant companion. At first, we went around with long faces because we missed Mary. Dad tried to help by bringing us a nice little grey cat.

One day when dad was out on the trap line, we got kind of hungry. Agnes asked me to cook something. I couldn't go to the ice house for meat because I was too small, so the next best thing was the cat. The fire was going in the big cast iron stove. We got the cat into the oven all right but when we shut the oven door, the cat started making a noise, and the stove began to smoke. We got scared and hid. When dad came back, he didn't punish us, but we sure missed our pet. I never tried to cook on my own after that, until I was quite a bit older.

That summer, dad started working for the missionaries, hauling supplies aboard the schooner *Our Lady of Lourdes*. It stopped at all the mission houses along the coast. The boat was to be wintered in Tuk, more than two hundred miles away by sea at the mouth of the Mackenzie Delta. So in early September, my dad left with the mission crew. The boat disappeared across the bay towards Amundsen Gulf and I didn't see my dad again until April.

When he and the crew returned, they weren't aboard *Our Lady of Lourdes*. They came in by dog sled. My father told us how the boat had got stranded in ice half way to Tuk because freeze-up came early. There were three dogs on the boat and dad built a small sled and loaded it with some supplies and hitched the dogs to it. They had to walk the rest of the way, he said, meeting many perils on the young ice and many moments of suspense during the wicked storms that blocked their path and increased their chances of getting lost. They didn't get to Tuk until October 16th.

Then dad told me to get my things. He said we were all going to go and chop loose the schooner, then go on to Tuk. We left by the same teams that dad and the crew had driven in with. Father Franche and Brother Kraut were in one team, dad, Agnes, Tommy and I were in another, and Father Biname and Brother Gosset in a third. Simon didn't need a team. He ran ahead of us all the way. That was the last I was to see of Paulatuk for many years.

I don't remember who sighted the trapped schooner first. It came into view on our seventh day out, locked fast in the Smoking Mountains ice pack near the shore of Franklin Bay. My dad and Father Franche made a check of the engine and put some fuel in from the oil cans we had brought with us, and Simon and the two Brothers chopped away at the ice with their axes. When we were finally free and out into open water, the ocean got pretty rough with the southwest wind blowing strong and nearly all of us were sick. Not my dad though. He was at the wheel in the pilothouse, steering a good course through the ice around Cape Bathurst and into Kugmallit Bay. Then, on the eastern shore, swept by the winds of the Beaufort Sea, we sighted Tuktoyaktuk.

Waving from the dock was my brother, Charlie, three years older than me. He was on holidays from school in Aklavik.

It was a busy place—Tuk, with the Catholic Mission House, the Anglican church, the Hudson's Bay Company store, Old Stan Peffer's store and lots of Eskimo and Indian families.

My dad got married again and he built a house on the

mission land. After that, when he wasn't out trapping or hunting, he'd be away in the East, with the mission boat, hauling supplies as far away as Spence Bay.

His absence made my stepmother cranky. She'd raise hell with everybody, including me. It scared me, so I'd go over to my new friend Mark Noksamia's house, or play with Uncle Edward Kikuak's children. Cousin Elizabeth was best because she always looked mad—even when she was happy.

Tommy and Charlie and I liked going down to the beach to watch the boats come in. Tuk was the last stop for the freight boats that moved slowly up the Mackenzie River all summer, bringing supplies from down South. The supplies were loaded at Tuk onto smaller boats that travelled the Arctic Coast, stopping in at all the tiny settlements. One of these was owned by a fur trader called L. F. Semmler. It was a paddle-wheeler called *The Distributer*. We'd see it coming in from the Beaufort Sea, and watch it being tied up next to Semmler's other boat, the one he called *Buck*. Stan Peffer owned a boat, too, that he hauled freight with.

On Sundays, Tommy and I used to play a game with the Anglican church bell. We would get up early and ring it, bringing people to church long before the service was due to start. The Reverend Thomas Omaok would come after us with a stick. But we were always too fast for the old minister. While the service was on, we would make funny faces through the church windows. Because we were Catholic children, complaints went to our priest, Father Delalande. He was a big, cheerful fellow who, like Father Franche, spoke Eskimo fluently. He would tell us to cut out the funny business, but I think he kind of got a kick out of it. It always seemed hard for him to keep from laughing.

A lot of people were out whaling that summer. When Reverend Omaok wasn't preparing his sermon or chasing us kids, he'd be out whale hunting, too. He used to land his kills close to our house. I would watch as Mrs. Omaok waddled down to the beach with her Ulu (Eskimo knife) and sometimes I would stay with her all day because she'd give me muktuk. She told me never to play with the church bell, but I didn't listen.

And then there was the Great Robbery. I don't recall who engineered it, but we stole the Anglican church collection—Tommy, Charlie and I. It was all small stuff—twenty-two dollars worth of pennies, nickels and dimes. Tommy and Charlie got most of the money. I had only one pocket in my pants, and couldn't carry much. Charlie and Tommy were caught right away, but I was the wise guy, hiding out till night-time. Then I went home and turned the loot over to my stepmother. I had no use for the stuff anyway—I didn't know what money was.

That fall, Tommy and Charlie went off to school in Aklavik and I was alone with Agnes again.

Then one morning a year later, it was my turn. My father packed a few things for me and we walked down to the dock together to wait for the mission schooner to come in and take me to school. I remember waving to him from the railing as *The Immaculata* pulled out into the bay and headed south towards Aklavik. I was crying. I didn't want to leave him. My dad wasn't at home that much, but when he was, I was always with him, watching him work, listening to his stories.

On the boat with me were two children I knew from Paulatuk, George and Florence Tardiff. George didn't want to go to school either, but Florence didn't mind. After a while, the three of us fell asleep. I don't remember anything of the trip down the Mackenzie until we got to Aklavik and a crew member pointed to the row boat and told us to get in. George and I were crying again as the little skiff neared shore. We could see the lights of the town to the right of the big two-storey schoolhouse and lights from other smaller buildings on the mission school property, and to the left, the shadows of houses scattered along the shore.

When we reached the little dock, Florence didn't even wait for the crew to tie up. She bounced excitedly out of the boat and raced up to the school. George was quick to get out, too. But he didn't run in the same direction. He ran and hid under a short wooden sidewalk that crossed a ditch. I remember seeing his tiny outline in the distance as the nuns dragged me into the school. George was jumping up and down, waving at them, and shouting, "You can't catch me! You can't catch me!"

But they did catch him. And he became a Grade I captive—just like me.

2

Playing with Girls is a Sin

All told, there must have been around eight hundred people living in Aklavik at that time. The rich families—they mostly worked for the Federal Government which had its Western Arctic headquarters there—lived in one or two-room houses built of lumber and heated with wood or oil. They were over near the hospital, and the Anglican school and cathedral, on the other end of town. A wooden sidewalk ran along in front of them, a wide ditch separating the sidewalk from the snow-packed road. Out back of the houses were the RCMP barracks, the police dog kennels, and the radio tower. Closer to our school was the Hudson's Bay Company store, the biggest of the stores in town, where the Indians and Eskimos who huddled in little huts and tents would sell their furs. Some Indians lived across the river and every day I'd see them crossing the ice on their way to jobs in town. The trappers all had happy expressions on their faces because the flat delta land on which Aklavik was located was rich with muskrat. In those days their pelts were worth as much as two dollars apiece.

The nuns in charge of us were Sister Bessant, Sister Soka, Sister Gilbert, and Sister Alice Rae, who I loved as much as my real mother. Sister Bessant was nice, too, but Sister Soka used a ruler on our hands and Sister Gilbert was hell-on-wheels for pulling ears, brushing our mouths with lye soap and whipping us with a watch chain. I could never understand how she could be so mean, and yet be very kind at the same time.

Sister Soka was my teacher. I couldn't catch on to the ABC's, and Sister Soka got a girl called Lena to show me. I was just a little guy, much smaller than Lena, but I wondered if she knew I thought she was pretty.

In the seat ahead of me was a boy named Danny Norris. Behind me was Freddie Carmichael. Whenever I wasn't eating my pencil, I was poking them with it. We had elastic slingshots, too, and every time the teacher turned her back, she was the target.

I was eating cooked food for the first time. I didn't like it and, like the other boys, I would sneak into the kitchen whenever I could and slip away with some frozen meat. We tossed our bones into the school yard and that's how it came to look more like a bone yard than a playground.

When anyone complained about the food, the nuns would make the complainer drink a whole can of cod liver oil, to do penance for committing something they called a venial sin. That was smaller than a mortal sin, and something else called a sacrilege was an ever bigger sin than a mortal sin.

You never went to Hell on venials.

There were as many girls as boys at the school. The girls' dormitory was on the top floor at one end of the main building, the boys' at the other end. We even ate in separate rooms.

We were told not to play with the girls, because that would also be a sin. I thought that was strange, because I had played with girls before I came to school. Now they were telling me I shouldn't touch them. I was taught not to look at girls, and not to look at dogs mating. But I had seen these things long before I went to school. I had seen people in the sex act when I was as young as three years of age. I knew exactly what it was, and how to do it, by the time I was six.

I was forever being scolded for eating with my hands. I didn't like using knives and forks and spoons. I'd drink my soup and rip the meat apart with my teeth. Then I'd wipe my mouth on my sleeves and wipe my hands on my clean, knee-length pants. Sister Gilbert put a stop to that.

My grades were somewhere between one and zero. But I was a good wood hauler. About five or six of us would drag loads of wood for the furnaces — four in the school and hospital, one in the parish house, one in the laundry, and one in the kitchen. They all used kindling.

When Hallowe'en came, we got to see our first movie — a silent one with Charlie Chaplin. It was scary, and a lot of us hid under the benches and cried. Brother Jack made things worse by coming in with a pumpkin with a candle glowing inside and holes carved to make the pumpkin look like an evil spirit. At that point I escaped into the arms of dear Sister Alice Rae.

When Sister Gilbert was in a good mood, she used to tell us stories from the newspapers she got sent up from the South. She told us about Adolf Hitler and Mussolini, Joseph Stalin and Churchill, and she said that the German war was going on strong and that Hitler was raising cain all over Europe and Africa. We prayed a lot that it would end soon.

There was a half hour of prayers in the morning, before and after breakfast. Dinner was at eleven o'clock, and there were prayers before and after that, too.

That fall we went on a picnic, camping overnight in the school shack about two miles into the snow-covered bush out back. I set a trap and caught a whisky-jack. I made a little fire, and burned the feathers off the big blue bird, then let it freeze, and ate it when it was frozen hard. It tasted like caribou liver.

That night someone told the legend of another Eskimo boy, Iliapaluk, an orphan who lived with his grandmother, Ananaa, in the bush country. They had a little house, Kutuk, of the kind that is dug into the earth with the roof at ground level. Iliapaluk was just a small boy. He used to snare rabbits with sinews, while the old woman fished with a bone hook. No one knew that this old woman possessed the magic power we call Angatkolik.

They had only the snares to count on for meat. One day, the boy came home and told his grandmother that someone had stolen them. They went to the nearby village to try and get them back, but whoever took the snares would not come forward. The old woman warned the village people not to make fun of a poor orphan boy. She told them she would give whoever took Iliapaluk's snares a chance to return them to him.

Still no one came forward, so they went back home, and the old woman told her grandson to go and hook a fish with roe in it. The boy did this, and the old woman cut the fish open, and took out the eggs. She told her grandson not to watch her for a moment. When the boy turned around, he saw she was covered with fish eggs from head to toe. She told him they were returning to the village, to get the snares.

When they arrived, she told the boy to call everyone out of their houses. When he had done this, the old woman began talking to them.

"I will touch all of you, one by one," she said. "If you are good people, do not be afraid. Only the liar will get hurt."

She then touched everyone, until she got to a man who suddenly dropped dead.

He was the thief. He had the snares.

Then the grandmother told the people, "Whatever you do, do not ever steal from an orphan who has no mother, and who fights hard to live. He only has those little strings to live on, and when you take them away, he can starve and die."

Story telling was a part of life in the North. My brothers and I were always competing to tell the best story. But we were no match for our grandfather. He was the greatest of them all. As he talked, he would light his pipe, and smoke "Old Chum" tobacco. Then he would pick up his drum, and sing. He would sing of Herschel Island in the Arctic Ocean, and tell of times that were good. He would sing of happiness after a successful whale hunt, about the big dances people used to have, of his young days, and his women, and of the medicine men of old.

One of my jobs at the school, with a boy called Douglas Dillon, was emptying the toilet pails. One day, we toppled down a twenty-foot bank on our way to the river to dump the slop. We came out looking like a couple of O'Henry chocolate bars. The outhouse at the end of the playground had sixteen seats, for over two hundred boys. Some of the seats were too big for the little boys, and they used to fall through them. I had the honour of being one of the lucky c 'es.

Christmas Week, we spent four days at the camp shack in the bush. We trapped muskrat, caught one cross fox, snared rabbits, climbed trees and chewed spruce gum. We also got a chance to see inside the girls' camp.

The toys we got for Christmas were great. I ran away from my first one, a rolling clown. It scared the Christmas spirit right out of me.

On New Year's Day there was a concert, and the RCMP were called in to take some drunks out of the school. They were trappers, and some people from town.

3

Saganna

The following summer at Tuktoyaktuk, my little sister Agnes got sick and died. I saw the missionaries take her from the house. I didn't want her to go. They said they were taking her to the hospital at Aklavik. I never saw her again. I loved her and I missed her a lot.

My adopted brother, Simon, tried to help me to forget about Agnes.

We used to go to Church, Simon and I, then we'd return home and hold our own service. Simon was always the priest, and I was always the altar boy. He'd put a blanket over his shoulders, and a tin can on his head, make the Sign of the Cross, and give me bannock for Holy Communion. Then he would start to preach. Silly things. How Adam and Eve stole a case of apples, and ran away from the Garden of Eden. How Martin Luther saw seven devils, and Henry the Eighth had eight wives and used to eat pork on Good Friday. He would baptize me a few times with ice cold water, then finish it off with a big slap, which was the Sacrament of Confirmation. Good old Simon—apart from playing, he was a good woodcutter, and a good fisherman.

The summer slipped by quickly and soon it was time to go back to school. The whole family set off by dog team towards Aklavik.

I had a toboggan of my own, pulled by two dogs. A good load, too. But going over the ice, I got tired after a while, so my dad took my load. Even then, it took me about an hour longer than the slowest team to reach the camp where we stopped that night. The next morning, we set out again and didn't reach our second camp until way after dark.

It was Lucas Neomatunas' place. We stayed there for a couple of days, jigging for lingfish, what the Eskimo people call Laush. From some herders in the area, we got fresh reindeer meat and some Tiparktark, which is half-rotten white fish. Dipped in whale oil, it's the treat of the North.

There were reindeer herders all over the Western Arctic in those days. What they were herding were not really reindeer at all, but caribou. They'd catch them wild and try to domesticate them. It was a government project to supply the people of the North with cheap caribou meat. But it has never met with much success.

Our next camp was Kittigazuit, an old abandoned Hudson's Bay fort at the mouth of the Mackenzie where, many years ago, hundreds of Eskimos were killed off by a 'flu epidemic after the southern whalers and traders came. I like the place, with its high-cut, treeless banks and sandy beaches and rocky outcrops. Not much is left of the old fort. Just a few wood-frame houses and thousands of whale skulls, scattered all over.

It is supposed to be a haunted fort. My dad went hunting, and Tommy, Charlie and Simon and I went exploring. We looked into an old ice house where they had thrown the bodies of the Eskimos who had died in that epidemic to await burial. They had to wait until summer came and the ground softened enough to dig the graves.

When I entered the ice house, I felt my bones chill. We could hear a funny whistling sound, but we couldn't see a thing. My dad's two dogs came in and I could see they were watching something. I wasn't afraid, but my stepmother was outside, screaming at us to come out. When we did, I could see the whole dog team was scared. The hair was standing up on their backs. I never knew what it was about that place, but there was something there we couldn't see.

Dad said that possibly it was the ghost of the man I was named after, Old Apakark. He was a medicine man who used to live in Kittigazuit. I am descended from a long line of medicine men.

Dad told us that people who camp in that icehouse know never to use the back room. There is a story about a man who went in there once. When he tried to pick up his tobacco can it kept moving away from him. Then he saw a figure standing beside him, not moving. When he tried to touch the figure, his hands went right through it.

We camped in one of the old houses that night. My dad got Charlie, Tommy and me together and told us a story, an old one, from his childhood back in 1905 on Herschel Island.

He said people used to kill the mentally sick then because they couldn't look after themselves and suffered too much in winter.

He said one of these insane creatures, to avoid capture, crawled under his mother's house, dug a hole like a dog and stayed there. At night when he was hungry or wanted tobacco, he would start to moan. My father said it was horrible and frightening—the noise he made . . .

My dad broke off the story and told us to go outside and walk around the house three times.

It was dark and we were nervous, peering this way and that. But we did as he told us. We came back and the story went on . . .

One night the creature's cries got weaker and weaker until all dad and his mother could hear was the lonely howl of the wind sweeping across the frozen Arctic

Ocean. The creature had died under the house . . .

Again my father stopped the story and told us to walk around the house three times.

We piled outside. The third time round, Tommy tripped me and ran. Thinking of the dead man, I was terror-stricken. I was all alone outside in the dark, and I couldn't move. But I had to. I didn't want them to know I was afraid. Finally I got up the courage to get myself going and in a moment I was safe inside and dad was starting up the story again . . .

One night he and his mother were sitting quietly in their house when the moaning began anew. The dead creature had come to life and was crying for water and tobacco. My father said they could hear the creature's footsteps mounting the steps of the front porch . . .

Again my father stopped the story and told us to walk around the house. But by this time we were all too afraid. We refused to budge. And so he went on . . .

His mother, he said, remembered the medicine man, Saganna. Saganna had told her when she was small that if she was ever frightened, she should pray to him and he would help her.

As the front door began to creak open, she started to pray. They could see the creature standing there in the shadow of the porch. His eyes were empty. His skin was hanging loose and his lips were curled back. There was blood coming from his gums where the skin of his mouth had dried up and cracked.

"Help me, I'm burning up," the creature moaned, shuffling slowly into the room. "I'm burning. Water. Give me water."

Dad said his mother prayed at the top of her lungs to Saganna. She was terrified. They were both terrified. And then it happened. As quickly as the creature appeared, he was gone. He never came back.

Saganna had answered the woman's prayers.

We all wanted to know more about Saganna, the medicine man. Dad said he had a caribou-skin parka with strange powers. The old people would spread it on the floor, kneel on the bottom edge to hold it down, then take hold of the shoulders in their hands and shake it.

They would call out the names of dead relatives and the relatives would talk to them.

He tried it once, he said, as a small boy, but he got scared when his dead uncle answered him, and he dropped the parka.

That same night, dad told us other stories, about when whaling men used to come to Herschel Island from the outside world on sailing ships. Some were four-masters. Others were six-masters. People started to kill each other then, he said, when the white men brought whisky and Hudson's Bay Company rum. But some old people died in a different way. They would get younger relations to kill them, dad said, to put an end to their suffering.

Breakfast the next day, early, was coffee, bannock and beans which I mixed with seal oil. A piece of whale blubber and frozen meat is a good breakfast, too. But most of the time, I would have muktuk (whale blubber) and coffee.

From Kittigazuit, we left for Homer's Creek and the reindeer herder's camp. It took us a day to reach it. On the way, we saw Michael Polk fly by with his sled deer. He was a happy little fat man from Lapland. His people lived just the way we did, and they were really friendly. When we reached Homer's Creek, we met Joseph Avik, an Eskimo herder from the east. We camped in a tar paper shack. Here again, at bedtime, dad told us a story.

It was about my Uncle Aleck Steffanson's hair-raising experience. Aleck was coming from somewhere west and he thought to look in at an old man who years ago lived in the very shack in which we were camped that night.

When he called out, no one answered. There was no light on in the house, no fire, no smoke from the stove-pipe. It was very dark, so Aleck went into the house and began feeling about in the dark. He thought no one was home. Then he tripped over something in the dark and he landed on it. The thing was hard. He lit a match and saw a frozen face looking at him. That scared the hell out of him and he took off up the river to report the death of the old man.

Thinking about that, I didn't sleep much that night. I was lying on the same floor where the old fellow died. I was glad to get out of there the next day.

Next stop was John Keevik's. I arrived last as usual, about an hour behind the rest. I met cousins Mary Amos, Margarette and Marion. Tommy, Charlie and I wrestled and played with the girls. Marion and I found out that cousins make the best friends.

Later we went hooking or ice fishing. There was a nice moon and we got quite a few Tiktalerk. When we got back that night, Mrs. Keevik cooked the fish, plus liver and eggs. She fried them all in grease, and I never tasted anything better in my young life.

We were there two days and it was hard to leave good people but we had to get to Bob Cackney's place. The Cackneys were a family from Tuktoyuktuk who had moved to the Mackenzie Delta to trap. The night we got to Bob's we had an Eskimo dance. I didn't know how to dance but I got up on the floor with my friend, Andy, who was a year older than me.

The next stop was another trapping camp, Old Irish's place. People called him Irish but he was Eskimo. His real name was Kogorkya, which means Northern Lights. A white man named Danes had a store there, and all he seemed to eat and sell were rotten apples. Old Danes charged my dad ten dollars for camping at his place, but my stepmother gave him hell and he gave the money back. He was tough with men, but soft on women. Or maybe he just got scared because of my stepmother's size.

I never knew my dad had any money, but dad had ten dollars in coins to give Danes. He got them out of an iron box he always carried with him. Until that night when I saw him open it, I never knew what the box contained. The box was twelve inches long, six inches wide and four inches high. It was full almost to the top with money. He was saving to buy a boat, he said.

We stayed at Jim Siksikark's place. It was nice there. Nobody ate rotten apples or charged us money. Jim had moose meat and lots of fish. White fish, jack fish and Tiktalerk. But the best thing he had was his little girl, Lita. She was almost the same size as me and we had a lot of fun sledding with a toboggan. The bank was high, right close to the house. And while we played, our parents got drunk. Jim had a brew pot and we stayed three days until the drinks ran out.

At the next stop, I met my real mom's dad and mother, Mr. and Mrs. Bennett Ningaksik, for the first time. We could only spend a little while with them though, because my stepmom wanted to get on to Aklavik. I cried when I had to leave my grandmother behind. I really loved her. Her Eskimo name was Ergiakyuk. It means mountain.

The portages were really rough, made worse by my slow team of two dogs, so Tommy helped me. We almost got into a fight when he started to use a chain to scare the dogs. He was stronger and older than me but I would always go down fighting, even if I couldn't win. I was all guts and tears. Simon Koblu wasn't having any trouble, though. He was running ahead of the dog teams. Had been ever since we left Tuk. That guy, he never ever got tired. I once saw him win a 200-yard dash with his hip-waders on.

At Bob Taylor's place, we had a good meal of frozen

muktuk and cooked muskrats, and we had some Eskimo ice cream which is like pemmican whipped up in fat. It's called Akutork. My stepmom could make the best aku-tork in the world. You take caribou meat and cut it into small pieces, then shred and dry it. Then you heat some fat over the stove until it becomes fluffy, and add the shredded meat and stir some more. Cool it, and you have akutork.

The next day we stayed at a trapping camp and had rabbit meat and soup for dinner. When we finally got to Aklavik, we had been on the move for over a month.

4

I Wasn't Bad all the Time

I arrived back at school dressed in warm reindeer skins and Sister Gilbert pushed me into the tub, telling me I smelled like muktuk. Later, as I struggled to put on the gray overalls that all of us children had to wear, I remember thinking that she stank under her armpits. But I never told her.

I felt like a Great White Hunter in the baby class. I was still in Grade 1. My new teacher was Sister Pulin. She was very gentle and never used a ruler on our hands like Sister Soka. Sister Soka couldn't teach school any more because her tits were leaking right through the front of her Grey Nuns' habit. Some of the older boys said that maybe she had had a baby. All I really cared about was to make good marks in cutting and hauling wood. I was not too bright, but I was a physical powerhouse for work.

That Christmas, boys and girls fainted from the heat inside the church during Midnight Mass while it was fifty below zero outside. I met Santa Claus who told me to study hard. When he told me that I was doing good work, cutting wood for the school, I got the suspicion I had met the fellow somewhere before. I had a hunch it was Barney Meniell, a radio operator at the local Aklavik station, dressed in Santa clothing. But I still wanted to believe in Santa and his little helpers. You should have heard my Christmas message. It sounded like warehouse inventory.

Dear Santa,

Please send me a big truck with wheels, also a big stocking with lots of candy, gum, chocolates, pretty toys, and lots of shells for my cap gun. Please also send me a new pocket knife to eat frozen muktuk and meat with. I have been a good boy all year but I swore once when I got into a fight with Joe Punch. Dear Santa, please forgive me because I lost that fight.

May God bless you
and your little helpers
Merry Christmas
From you know who.

On Christmas morning, I got a toy truck as a present, and a stocking full of goodies. The Christmas spirit didn't stay long though. When we came back from the bush camp, there was a fight in the boys' room. A boy named Pierre from Arctic Red River was trying to drive a nail into the head of a Coppermine boy named Patrick Natit. Two other Eskimo boys who had learned to swear had their hair cut off. Sister Gilbert and another nun shaved their heads bald and put dresses on them, and then they were paraded before the girls and boys. The two lucky guys were Charlie Steen and Adam Kupan. I thought I'd better watch out and not swear. I could just imagine myself bald-headed and in a dress.

New Year's Eve came.

We could hear guns going off all over town. The New Year's concert was full as usual, with a mid-day show for the school children and an evening show for the townspeople. My grandfather was there. It was easy to see him with his tight green tam pulled over his bald head. Father Coty got me into one of the acts as a drummer boy. In a gold-braided uniform, I felt as tall as Mackenzie King, the Canadian Prime Minister. I had another reason for being proud. I was now in Grade II.

Sister Kristoff, the superior of the nuns at the school, found out I liked raw, frozen meat from the kitchen. She used to let me have some. They'd sometimes serve us raw whitefish eggs, too. I'd come away from those meals licking my fingers, with my mouth watering for more.

One day the nuns took us to the North Star Inn for a free lunch. It was some treat, my first time in a white man's café. The baker at the Inn was Happy Nantis. At least, that's the name we knew him by. He had a son, Jerry, in school who used to bring cookies and pastries his dad made and give them to the teachers for us lucky boys.

Easter came, and I saw the first painted eggs I had ever seen in my life. The shells looked too beautiful to crack, but the insides were too good to leave, so we ate them.

That spring I got into a scrap with two Indian boys from Fort Good Hope—Ernest and John Kochilac. I got a licking from John first and then I got a good beating from Ernest. And then Sister Gilbert entered the picture and punished us, by making us box with a post. We boxed with that post for an hour before we had to beg on our knees for her pardon. The fight started when they called me a muktuk huskie. Muktuk was all right but a huskie is a dog, and I showed them what a huskie dog can do. I lost one tooth and got a black eye. John had a bloody nose and Ernest had a black eye, too. And all three of us were crying. But it didn't end there because the two boys had an uncle in the school, named Yessante Kochilac. He came after me for fighting with John and Ernest and was making mush out of me when my brother—good old Tommy—came to the rescue. He whipped the living hell out of that big Indian tomahawk-grabber. It was strange. Although we were good friends with the Indians, we fought them at the same time. I think we must have been young versions of the old-timers.

That summer my father came to town behind the wheel of a big, 37-foot, red and green scow with a 50-horsepower Buick car engine. He'd bought it out of the savings in that big metal box of his. It had taken us a month to get from Tuk to Aklavik by dog team but we made the return trip on dad's new scow in fourteen hours.

At Tuk, I tried to get up to my old tricks again, but I couldn't reach the Anglican Church bell. The Reverend Omaok had cut the rope. So instead I took a pail and filled his dinghy with water. He caught me red-handed and threw me, clothes and all, into the drink. He reported everything to my stepmother and she used a pair of rubbers on my most natural spot. After that, I was good for a while until I pulled the Reverend's fish net up on the beach.

There were lots of fish in it and they were flopping all over the sand. I turned some of our dogs loose and soon there were five big dogs fighting over the fish on the beach. When the Reverend Omaok arrived, he and I pulled the dogs apart and tied them up. Then he turned to me and asked if I had seen who had pulled the net up.

I tried to look innocent but he gave me a look and said, "Ilani Amaman Erkuaktalasigatin"—which means "your mother is going to spank you sometime."

He must have guessed.

I wasn't bad all the time. Just mischievous. Often, I would watch over my sisters and my little brother, George. I even learned how to mix milk for my baby sister, Mona. Mona was born deaf and couldn't talk. She was also a little blind, but I loved her just like the rest.

That summer, the trappers were getting good prices for their muskrat pelts and a lot of people were away trying to trap as many as they could in the Delta. Whaling was good, too. I'd go down to the harbour to watch the hunters come in. Some boats would have four big whales in tow.

There was a big square dance to celebrate. Ikey Bolt did the calling. His favourite was the "Red River Jig". But I had another name for it—"Two Cylinders". That's because it had a beat like a two-cylinder Frisco Standard engine.

Albert Ludette was first up on the floor, with Bessie Cackney. Then Simon got up and started shaking around. Someone had paid him two bits to jig. The whole place shook with laughter at his antics. There was another dance, called "I'll Hold You In My Arms". It meant nothing to me. The only girl I had ever held in my arms up to then was my baby sister. The dance ended with "Home Sweet Home", which sounded sad, and people started leaving. Big tall Red Walker, the RCMP constable, was checking around. I saw boys taking girls home so I walked home a girl called Emilie Voudras. Sometime after that, Tommy tried to tell me what a girl was really for, but I already knew.

The next five years of school were pretty much like the first two. Nothing made much sense to me. I felt I'd sooner be a trapper than learn what they were trying to teach me. I liked reading, but I wasn't much of a writer. I couldn't even spell "arithmetic" right. About all I enjoyed was the chance to tend my trapline with the other boys in the bushes across town after classes in the afternoon. We would go there and make an open fire, cooking our own meals and making strong black tea. Later we would take our catches of muskrats and rabbits down to the basement and skin them. We would put the skins on stretchers. The rabbit skins we dried for use as duffles.

I was closer to wildlife than I was to the three R's.

Even at an early age, I knew the ground squirrel was a sign of spring, the big timber wolf meant caribou, white mice meant many foxes, seals were a sign of the polar bear and the otter was a sign of fish.

Once I watched two white mice by an old grave. They

were eating green roots from the ground. One of them looked up at me. It had a piece of shrub in its paws. It somehow sensed that I wouldn't hurt it and went right on eating. I touched the mice and handled them a while, then let them go. These little creatures knew a friendly voice, they could sense a friendly human, their wild instincts were unspoiled, their senses were clear.

The summer I was nine, I got a new set of clothes for trapping and I was never more proud of myself. My dad returned from the East on the mission boat with fresh seal meat aboard and my stepmother cooked some seal guts with meat and we ate it with raw seal blubber.

That same summer there was lots of excitement. Twenty-five children from mission school spent the holidays with us, attending what the Fathers called "summer camp". I don't know where their dads and moms were. Some nuns and brothers from the school looked after them and Father L'Holgouach was their spiritual leader. Those children prayed so much! If anything had happened to them, they'd have gone straight to Heaven.

There was a big surprise in August. The RCMP schooner, *St. Roch*, called in at Tuk. It had come all the way from the other side of Canada. A man called Larsen was in the pilothouse. I was told he had set some kind of record for sailing the northern seas. But I knew better. My dad was the champ when it came to sailing the Arctic. He had put more waves and ice under him than any man.

It was a time of happiness. But it didn't last long.

Changes were beginning to show at home—changes that disturbed me deeply. Every year when I came home from school, things seemed worse than the year before. My father was going away on the boat more and more, and my stepmother—finding herself alone—had taken to drinking heavily.

She was all right when dad was with her, but when he

was away—and often he'd be gone for a month at a time
—she would get mean and kick me and my brothers out
of the house. I think she suspected dad had women in the
places he visited in the East.

One day a nice girl called Nora came to the house and
my stepmother jumped up and chased her with a broom,
calling her every name under the Northern Lights. She
was that way with other strange women, too.

One year when I came home, I learned that my
stepmother had almost killed Simon with an axe. Bishop
Trocellier, who was the head of the Roman Catholic missionaries in the Western Arctic, Father Delalande and my
father, when he returned from the East, somehow kept
Simon alive. Because of the important part my father
played in mission work, the church allowed nothing to
happen to my stepmother. She wasn't put in jail.

At times my father seemed to grow weary of me. I
talked too much and asked too many questions and he
would say, "You should pray more and talk less." But
most of the time I think he was proud of me because I was
becoming a good hunter and trapper and always thought
of my little brothers and sisters wanting meat.

One day my stepmother threw a big rock at me and I
ran away for a few days. Dad kept some pilot biscuits
under the porch and I would sneak home and grab some,
then run back to my hideout, which was a nice cool place
under an old scow belonging to Emilie Voudras' father.

The Reverend Omaok's wife found me sleeping under
there one morning and she gave me some bread. After
that, the old minister would come himself with dried meat
and whale blubber for me to eat. Rotten oranges, apples
and grapefruit thrown into Kugmallit Bay by the Hudson's Bay Company made good eating, too.

Good old Tommy and Charlie and I made up our
minds to make some money. Tommy told us we could
find work with L. F. Semmler. His boat was in and we got

jobs unloading supplies. I made eight dollars and went out and bought four cans of honey and candy. Tommy and Charlie bought chocolates and sweet biscuits. We cached them all inside an old shallow grave built of logs. Our stuff was stored among the bones of a body that had been buried there years before. We figured that when our stepmother finally kicked us out for good, we'd have something to eat, if nothing else. That grave became a regular storehouse for the three of us. Sometimes we'd even take muktuk and dried meat there. The diet of muktuk and honey wasn't too bad.

One day down by the shore, Tommy, Charlie and I met our grandfather's brother, Abraham Teriglook. He was one hundred years old. He told us a story out of his early life, way back in 1870.

He was travelling with a friend. They got caught in a big storm and his partner froze. There was no meat, so he cut a piece off his partner's leg. He cooked it and that piece of meat saved his life. He told me it tasted like pork.

He told us the story of another man, a little older than himself, who left Alaska with his wife way back, heading East to follow the caribou. His wife got sick so he built her a little sheltering tent and told her to stay there so that he could find her when he came back from hunting.

He left her what food he had, took his muzzle-loader and two dogs and headed out looking for caribou. He was used to the barren lands, but he got lost in the mountains. The summer was hot, and at night the mosquitos were very thick and they blinded him. Two months out, he had to eat his two dogs. At last he found the trail back. He thought of his wife, hoped she was okay, and that she had killed the dogs he left her for meat. Eventually he saw a small white spot in the distance, which he knew was his tent. When he reached it, there was just one dog alive. It had eaten the others. He looked into the tent, and his wife was dead. She had starved to death. Her body was dried by the sun and the flies had got to her. He cried out of pity for his wife, thinking how she had suffered and waited for him. He covered his wife with some wood, left her stuff beside the body, and went on his way.

Our little female husky, Kumak, had fourteen pups. Kumak was tied not far from the house, and I couldn't find my little brothers and sisters I was supposed to watch out for. The pups were scattered all over the place and when I found my little brothers and sisters, they were all sucking Kumak's milk. Milk is milk, but I have never heard of pasteurized dog's milk. When the children found out I was watching they all took off laughing. I put the pups back with their mother. When I told my dad, he said it was nothing to worry about, it was good milk.

One day the children put my stepmother's best bloomers on Old Brownie, our biggest dog. I couldn't get them off, I was laughing so hard. Just then mum saw me. She thought I was trying to put them on Brownie instead of trying to take them off. She went for her broom, and I ran for it.

When she wasn't in a temper, my step-mum could be really nice. I did love her in a way, but she always told me I knew too much. I remember at the age of two sucking my sister's breasts, but I remember someone else too, before that, a nice big woman, her breasts against my face wiping tears from my eyes. Who was that? Maybe my stepmother was right. I might have known too much.

5

Whipped by a Nun

Each fall, the arrival of *The Immaculata* meant the beginning of a new school year. I'll never forget the start of the trip in 1946, the year I was nine. Early in the morning, the nuns herded all of us children down to the dock to wait for the schooner. It was late as usual, and by the time it came into view, we were running all over the dock, playing games. I had to laugh at the antics of the nuns as they tried to keep our little group together. They sounded like a bunch of geese overhead, flying north for the summer. When the schooner finally reached the little dock and tied up, those nuns were fit to be tied themselves. They calmed down when all of us were on board, and they must have felt heavenly thankful that we managed it safely because as the schooner backed away from the dock to begin its voyage down the Mackenzie, the nuns began singing Ave Maria. And it was very beautiful. I had goose bumps and I had trouble holding back the tears, it was such a lovely parting ceremony. On the way to Aklavik, we stopped to pick Akpik, berries we called "nickels" because they were about the size of nickels. We filled about eight, sixty-pound tin cans with them before continuing on our way.

Most of the time, school was pretty monotonous, and I still couldn't figure out why I had to waste so much time at

35

it. But there are some things that happened that I remember very well.

Every fall there were some new boys at school, from Fort Good Hope and Arctic Red River south of Aklavik, and some others from out in the Delta. I remember when Gabriel Harris came, he couldn't speak much English. All he could speak was Slavik Indian.

We talked by sign and expression of face.

I had a bow and arrow which he wanted badly. He did the best he could with his few words.

He said, "Gimmie shoot it, me gimmie you num num." This meant, "Give me your bow and arrow, and I'll give you candies."

I remember learning to skate. At least I learned how to put the skates on before landing on my back on the ice. I was out skating one day when I heard a cry for help. It was Fred Wolkie, a cripped boy from Baillie Island. I pulled him out of a hole in the ice where he was stuck up to his chest. It was about sixty below outside, and the winter water wasn't what you would call warm. Wolkie and I were friends after that, but nobody else cared for him because of his stiff arms.

That same day somebody shot me in the mouth with an arrow and I went into school with it stuck in my top lip.

We were always forced to sit through prayers to the very end. Sometimes they would last an hour. It sure caused trouble for little Harold Clark. He would squirm and bounce, trying to hold his water, then wet the floor where he knelt. Even I had that happen to me a couple of times, and it was kind of embarrassing to get up after prayers and walk away from a wet patch on the floor.

One Christmas, I was put in the concert, in the Virginia Reel dance act. For partners we had boys dressed in wigs. My little madame was named Adam. Adam and Eve rolled into one bundle. The whole town was watching when you swung your partner and his long johns peeped out from under his dress. We had to do the same act over again on New Year's Eve.

A boy from Arctic Red River showed me how to play straight poker and black jack. I wasn't a bad gambler, but I wasn't as good as our Reverend Sister Gilbert. She gambled with a punch-card, making people pay up to two dollars and fifty cents a punch. You punched a card and if your number came up, you won. She made a lot of money on it and she said it was all for charity. Well, you know, I never believed her.

I was learning more and more about girls, and it was starting to get me into trouble. One day we were carrying fish to the kitchen. Some girls were teasing me and calling me Big Toenail. I shouted back a name, "Three-by-one", because the neck of one of the girls looked one inch thick and three inches long. It was William Clark's girl-friend and we got in a fight over it. I got the best of him but he got his big uncle, Billy Cardinal, to beat the hell out of me. I got a licking but it didn't break my habit of playing around with girls.

Sister Tebear, from the girls' side of the school, accused George Tardiff, Charlie Steen, Adam Kupan, and me of sinning with some girls in the basement of the school. The basement was a big one, and the fresh vegetables we got from Fort Smith and other places were kept down there in great big bins. There were new potatoes, cabbages, turnips, carrots, lettuce and radishes. Some of these were grown in a garden beside the parish house during the summer. In the winter, we would have to sort them out, but the girls did most of that. We told Sister Tebear we were all out in the playground at the time we were supposed to have been sinning in the basement, but she wouldn't buy it.

We were strapped to a bed and whipped with a three-foot watch chain made of silver. Sister Gilbert gave the whipping, and Father L'Holgouach okayed it. My back was bleeding but something else burned more. Shame. It was branded in my brain. The silver chain has never left my mind. Even to this day you can see the scars on my back. When I touch my back I feel the pain in my mind.

From the winter trapping money one year, the big boys put together enough money to buy a brand new movie sound projector. We had a double-feature show that Easter—Roy Rogers and Dale Evans were in one, Gene Autry in the other. Later in the spring, we had films of the war. Hitler, Stalin, Roosevelt, Chamberlain, Churchill and President De Gaulle were all shown in the same feature. We also saw boxing fights, with Joe Louis, Joe Walcott, Jack Dempsey, Jack Sharkey, Gene Tunney, Max Baer, Max Schmelling, Tony Galente and Archie Moore.

Sister Tebear would have given any of them a run for their money, though. She was about five-foot-four and weighed three hundred pounds, and could punch out any boy in the school. When she hit someone, he stayed down and out. I bet she could have licked Joe Louis and Jack Dempsey in the same ring.

One winter Brother Dellill killed a young dog on the mission team. It was taken to our cellar to skin. The fur was to be used for mitts. Jack Koudlark and I did the skinning. It was the first dog I had ever skinned. It was fat. The meat looked good but we had caribou and reindeer meat so we just threw it away, then we stretched the skin to dry in the basement. When it was good and dry, we took it to an old Eskimo woman to tan and cure the hide. She used baking soda to take the smell away, then rubbed caribou brains on the skin side, then let it dry some more. Later she scraped and tanned it till it was nice and soft. She made a beautiful pair of black and white spotted fur mitts.

One year after Easter we got hell for fighting with boys from the Anglican School. We heard one day that James Stewart, Willie Kindie, and another boy wanted to fight with three of us from the Roman Catholic School. The message was passed to us by a girl. I didn't know anything about this deal until William Clark brought it up. Clark picked Freddie Rioet, and he also picked me. I was stronger than them, and I was dumb enough to go to the Hudson's Bay Company store for the battle royal.

Stewart and his gang showed up and Stewart asked me if I wanted to fight, and it started. I sent James, bloody and crying, into a rack of clothes, then went after Kindie. In the end, I found I'd damn near taken on three boys at once. Jim MacDonald got hold of me and said, "OK, champ. That's enough. You got 'em licked."

I became a hero. But not for long. A few days later I went to the store alone, and there were twenty or thirty boys from the other school waiting for me, and they tried to push me around. I knocked a few down and ran. They gave up after chasing me about a mile and a half. But I had to go back to school sometime and they were waiting for me. This time they caught me and at least ten boys with boards and sticks gave me the licking of my life. I ended up in the police station, and they couldn't believe I was alone against all those Anglican schoolboys. They picked on me for two things, because I was a Roman Catholic and because I was a damn Eskimo.

At last spring would come, revealing lush green timbers and thousands of grassy lakes in the Mackenzie Delta. In places, gas would bubble up from under the ground and I would chop through the ice to get at it. When it started coming through my hole, I'd set it on fire. The air pressure from under the ice made it look like a big jet flame.

That same gas, later in the Fifties, was to attract hundreds of petroleum explorers from the South. They were to move into Aklavik with their white crews. A real rough, drunken bunch, they put up high drilling towers all over the Arctic to suck up the gas they knew was under there.

When the ice was gone, we left by barge to load wood for next winter's use. It was heavy work and the spruce gum made us all sticky. Brother Vachan, Brother Class, and some hired men chopped wood during winter and we'd haul it away to the school each spring. I liked the fresh spring air and the Delta water, free of ice. It was different from some places higher up near the coast, Kittigazuit, for instance, where the ice floes stayed around all summer.

6

A Man—Aged Twelve

On the trips to the coast, I was beginning to take an interest in exploring the countryside, looking for sites where people camped many years ago. Walking along the shore again at Kittigazuit, I saw arrowheads made of bone, some as long as ten inches. There were smaller ones, too, with barbed ends. And there were harpoon heads and bone knives and bone sinkers for nets.

Especially interesting was a hill I found—about two hundred feet high. When I walked closer I could see it was a hill of whale bones—piled one on top of the other. They looked as if they had been dumped there thousands of years before. Nearby were many old burial grounds. In some of them, you could still see the kayaks, harpoons, knives, and sleds with bone runners that had belonged to the people buried there. They were covered with logs, weather-worn and decayed. There were also many ground squirrels, what we call siksik. I trapped some and my dad cooked the meat. They tasted mossy.

There were night-time stories from dad, about old people long ago. He told us how they used to bury their medicine men. They would build a platform, a big one, and wrap the dead medicine man in caribou skin and place him on the platform so his spirit would be free to help his people. Hunters would make offerings and pray to the medicine man for good hunting . . .

But at school I wasn't doing so well. I was the class dummy. I really liked geography. I liked art, too, but when I drew horses they always ran on stiff legs, and my drawings of lions always smiled. One day I got caught drawing a little devil-figure and had to stay after class, but I guess I made amends because I got a Sacred Heart badge for being holy.

Christmas dinner that year was something special, served at school on white, lace-trimmed table cloths. The turkey was served on china plates and the real silver, used only on special occasions, was brought out.

We had ice cream and got to sit across from the girls. What more could an eleven year old want? A girl named Pauline and I had our eyes glued together during grace. We seemed to pray to each other instead of to the Cross on the wall.

A month after that, I got word that my adopted brother went out on the trap line without telling anyone he was sick. Poor old Simon. He would never complain. He came back and died at home.

That same winter Tom was suspended from school. He had smashed some benches and windows with a base-ball bat. And he had taken the mission tractor and trailer. They punished him by making him run almost fifty-five miles. I don't know how tired he was, but it hurt me. No one should be punished that bad.

We got out of school early that year, sometime in April. The first thing we did was bury Simon's axe. It weighed forty pounds, with a steel blade and a brass handle.

Hunting was good that spring. I had a twelve-gauge shotgun and I went out with my dad and two brothers. For three nights, we went without sleep. It was worth it. We got over five hundred muskrats. Coming back, my paddle slipped out of my hands, over the side of the canoe, and into the water. When we reached home I crawled up the bank and when my stepmom tried to feed me, I fell with my head into my plate of soup. I was that tired.

A few days later, Tommy and I went out again, just the two of us.

There's an old Eskimo legend that if two people take the same action at the same time it's a sign that something bad will happen. Tommy and I stopped on a piece of ice and we both took a leak at the same time.

"Let's go home," Tommy said, "something bad will happen."

I didn't believe him and we kept on hunting.

About an hour later, when I was trying to hook a muskrat we had shot, I heard Tommy holler. I looked around quickly, and I saw that the hook had caught Tommy, just above his right eye. It had just about pulled it out.

It scared the life out of me, and we turned for home and paddled full blast all the way, some five or six miles. That incident made me a believer in legendary warning signs.

According to these legends, an owl call over camp is a sign of death, a single brant goose, calling as it flies overhead, means danger. If you keep a dream, vision or strange experience to yourself instead of sharing it, your conscience will bother you and eventually kill you.

In the old days when people wanted luck for hunting, they would put an offering in a medicine man's grave. Acts of kindness to orphan children or to old people also brought luck. Some tribes used to burn a piece of fur from the type of animal they wanted to hunt, for luck, and the burning fur was also supposed to chase away the evil spirits of the air. To change bad weather to good, Eskimos would make a big fire and burn an old shoe of caribou skin.

By July that year, my dad and my two brothers and I

had close to twenty-five hundred muskrats and lots of ducks and geese. The meat we didn't eat we put in our ice house for later use. Then we left for Aklavik to trade the furs.

On the way, we stopped at Old Joe Weichen's place. Old Joe was a funny bugger and a funny thing happened that time. He always had a big brewpot on and his pet cat was always hanging around. This time, we couldn't find the cat but he thought it was running around somewhere.

That day he invited my dad and mom and some of the other trapper families in for a party. The party was going strong and everyone was high on the homebrew. All at once, Joe put his arm into the brew and his eyes started bulging out like a couple of big cups.

"Jeee-sus! Here's my cat!" he shouted.

Then he started wringing the brew out of the cat and back into the barrel where it had drowned. A lot of stomachs turned when the guests found out they were drinking Black Cat Brew, and I don't think anybody ever accepted another party invitation from Old Joe.

Somebody said he used to take the fermented fruit from his brew barrel and rinse it out from inside an old pair of socks. Sometimes, they said, he would use his underwear legs as a wine press.

Pot brew was a favourite in the North. The main ingredients were malt extract and yeast, with dried fruit, rice and beans for a base.

Take a two-hundred-pound wooden keg butter barrel, fill it half-full with about five gallons of hot water, pour in fifteen pounds of sugar, six pounds of malt extract, ten pounds of raw rice, four pounds of dried apricots, six fresh potatoes, sliced to ferment better, then stir until the hot water is brown and sweet. Fill the barrel with cold water until the brew is lukewarm, mix eight packs of yeast in warm water with a little flour and pour the yeast mixture into the eight or ten-gallon brew in the barrel. The cover of the barrel should be tightly secured, with just a small vent to let a little bit of air escape. Wrap the barrel in caribou skins to keep it warm, and leave it to ferment.

Trappers would set off for their lines dreaming of the home brew they would come back to, but it killed a lot of them in the end.

On July 21st, I turned twelve years old.

A few weeks later, I was back at school, being accused of sinning again with girls in the basement of the school. There were two of us in the basement with four girls. All we were doing was throwing potatoes and having fun, but Sister Cote gave us hell. She lined us boys up against the wall and showed us what she thought of girls.

"Winnie, Wilma, Rosie, Mary, Jean, Marjie, Lucy, Annabelle . . . " she shouted. "This is what I think of them . . ."

She spat on the floor and stamped her foot on it.

She didn't have to do that. I was still too young to be having any serious thoughts about girls. And anyway, I was too holy. Sometimes I'd steal into the chapel and pray like hell, all by myself.

* * * * *

The following spring, dad had a stroke. Half of his body was paralyzed—half of his face, his right arm, his right leg. He couldn't talk properly any more. I was told he suffered it while trying to haul in the anchor of the *Our Lady of Lourdes*. The anchor was a heavy one attached to a 300-foot chain. I was twelve, and my father's condition was so bad I had to become a full-time provider. He couldn't work any more, so I was discharged from school.

Part Two

The old days are gone

7

You'd Better Have a Gun

In 1943, watching the arrival of the old freight paddle-wheeler, *The Distributer*, after spring breakup was still the big event for the Eskimo. From the dock at Tuk, we could see the smoke belching from the old ship's stack when it was still twenty-five miles out, making its way slowly along the Arctic Coast from the Mackenzie River in the west. All winter long we used to think of the oranges, apples, candies, or maybe the pair of socks we might be able to buy. Some trappers would think of the new trap or snow knife they wanted to have, but I always thought of the oranges when *The Distributer* came in from the South. In those days, I was so young I didn't know what money was.

Seven years later when I left school in Grade VI to look after my family, money still had no meaning for me. Hunting and trapping did though, because the day had arrived for me to help provide. My dad was almost helpless after his accident and he drank a lot. So did my stepmother, so my brothers and I would go out hunting every day for food for the table.

Tommy and Charlie would hunt together and I'd go off by myself in a small canoe. I had a .22 Winchester, my old twelve-gauge shotgun, and a .303 Winchester lever action. Funny things would still happen though.

Tommy came home one day covered with lice. He'd

been in town and picked them up. They were crawling all over him. We shook out his sweater over a barrel and put a four-pound can of jam on top of the lice to kill them. But there were so many, they made the can move. Lye and green liniment took care of Tommy's problem.

Sometimes I went out hunting whale with Uncle Tom Kalinerk. We got quite a few. It's fun, but it sometimes takes patience.

We would anchor the boat in a few fathoms of water, waiting for a school to show up. On a clear day you could see them coming for twenty miles, the spouts of water spraying into the sun. The whales can hear voices from a long distance, so we would make no noise in the boat. Throwing a harpoon takes practice, but sometimes we would not kill the whales, just sit by and watch them. One day in a small bay we watched a mother whale have two young ones. We stayed quiet while she kept pushing the little three-foot babies up out of the water until they learned how to breath on their own, and to swim. It took only a short time.

When summer came, the whole family went out with Bob Taylor's family on a whale hunt. My dad was only half alive but he made the trip. Near White Fish Station, we stopped at a little place I call Coconut Island. There was a big bottle of homemade beer on the scow. There weren't any whales around, so a party started on board. Mom and Mrs. Taylor got feeling quite high after a while and they decided to go and pick berries. In their condition, they couldn't use the long, narrow gangplank, so they decided to go ashore in an eighteen-foot canoe. They moved it into position between the scow and shore and started to get into it. And that's when the fun began. My stepmother, with Mona, George and William, managed all right. But when Mrs. Taylor tried stepping into the canoe, she didn't quite make it. Eva Taylor, Jessie Kaglik, Agnes, Lawrence, Tom, Bob Taylor and myself...we

were all watching. Over it went in three feet of water. The
two women went under with one big splash. So did the
children.

The women were big, weighing at least two hundred
pounds each. I fell on my back laughing, and so did the
others. The women crawled ashore crying, and that
looked even funnier.

In the meantime, William, the youngest of my brothers, nearly drowned. When the canoe tipped, he didn't
show up till Tommy went and fished him out.

My grand-dad tied up his schooner next to the island,
too. He was also drunk, and that same day he tried crawling along the plank that connected *his* boat to shore. He
got about four feet of the way when the plank tipped
over. In went grandpa. The water was just deep enough to
cover him, and when he bobbed to the surface, his fa-
mous green tam was still perched on top of his head.
Uncle Simon Bennett heard the splash and came out and
called to his sons, Walter and Fred, to bring the canoe.
They wouldn't, so Uncle Simon took a running start and
jumped overboard to rescue grandpa. Another great
splash! It was sure exciting. Seven people in the cold
water in one single day.

One day I went hunting ptarmigan alone. It was still
summer, but getting on towards fall. It was getting dark
at night. I had shot a few birds and was heading home
late. In the gathering darkness, I walked slowly and quietly. I heard a wolf's call, the kind they give when they see
something to hunt. My rifle was only a .22 calibre, but I
felt safe because I had my hunting knife. A knife can't fail
where a gun can jam. I walked, crouched low, so I could
see the line of the hills against the sky. Then I stopped to
listen. I heard a brushing sound and I saw two wolves. Big
ones. The sound I heard was their young pups playing. I
knew enough to stay downwind. I knew nothing could follow me unless it caught my tracks. When I got home, my

dogs were barking like mad, and when I got up next morning I could see wolf tracks only a hundred feet from the dogs.

I spent most of that fall fishing. I had eleven nets out before freeze up and I got thousands of fish. I put them away in the icehouse with the ducks and geese and whale heads. When winter came, I had sixteen nets under the ice, and I would check them twice a day. By that time, I was the only one at home able to cut wood, fish, hunt and trap. Tommy had gone away, looking for a wife or something, and Charlie was somewhere else, too.

At Christmas time, I went to Paulatuk to hunt with the Rubens boys and Garret Markes, David John, and Alex and Sam Green. One afternoon, I tried to make it back to the village ahead of the others. I was going along all right, but suddenly my seven dogs smelled caribou and struck out on a fast chase in the dark. But it's no use hunting caribou at night with no moonlight, and within minutes we were lost.

I looked for stars but it was cloudy. I decided to head southeast across a snow drift. I travelled on into the night, just hoping I was going in the right direction. When I thought I was about half-way across Darnley Bay, I turned southwest. I thought it odd that there wasn't any land in sight after five hours. It was pitch dark and I had no blankets, no food, no primus stove, and I was tired. I made a little snow house, put in five dogs and went to sleep among them. It was warm in there.

When daylight came, I crawled out and looked over the hill. I was not five hundred yards from the Catholic Mission House at Paulatuk. All the others were there having coffee. They made a lot of jokes about my misadventure. And I learned a good lesson—always travel prepared and take time to think first.

If it hadn't been for my dogs, I might have frozen to death. My lead dog, Whitey, knew we were only a few hundred yards from Paulatuk. He was puzzled when I made camp. He cocked his head because he couldn't understand why we were staying there. Dogs can often sense things that humans can't. You have to know when they are trying to tell you something. When you're travelling and your dogs stop and the fur is up on their backs, when they give a low whine, like a whispered growl, you'd better have a gun handy. Dogs know the scent of danger. Wolf or bear, they can pick them out. When a team gets excited and fast, it's a sign of caribou, maybe white fox. You can tell by a dog's bark whether it is a polar bear or a dog team coming into camp. If you are kind to your dogs, they are kind to you. They will protect you.

When I was too small to hunt alone, I used to take an old dog named Brownie with me. I used to make him carry my catch on his back pack. Many times I used Old Brownie to warm my frozen toes and fingers after I rubbed them with seal oil. When I'd fall asleep, he would lick my hands and feet clean.

When you are putting together a team of dogs you first train the lead dog, then the spare leader, then you mix in young dogs who know how to behave, and finally you select and train the wheel dog, the strongest and most hard-working of them all. Dogs learn from each other how to behave. They mostly watch and follow the leader. When a team driver gives voice or signal commands, the dog next to the leader learns how to answer by following the lead dog.

I got about 450 muskrats in the month of March. The price then was somewhere around two dollars or two dollars and fifty cents. I had worked hard to get them. Charlie came home and my dad sent him to Nagsoyak to sell them. Charlie didn't show up for a few days and when he finally did, he had less than fifty dollars worth of supplies and no money in his pockets. He had lost the muskrats in a poker game. He was in the soup up to his ears.

That July, I turned fourteen years old. I could throw a 200-pound anchor ten or twelve feet out from the front of our scow. To the Eskimo, I was almost a full man. In the Eskimo culture, a man is at his best at seventeen or eighteen. He is considered old at twenty-seven or thirty, and forty is really old. Very few grow older than that.

In the fall, after the last big whale hunt, my dad had to give the Missionaries our house at Tuk, plus five hundred dollars. I don't know why, but he did. This, after he had worked for the church for over twenty years. All those years and he ends up in debt after being paralyzed by a stroke.

We had to find another place, so we moved into a little driftwood cabin outside of town.

He said it was no use complaining.

"I suffer for Christ and He suffered for me," was all my dad would say.

I couldn't believe it—the richest Church in the world coming down on a poor crippled man who had served that long. I am not against the Church but I think they should have considered his long years of service. My dad had started to drink, but look at the long partnerships. My dad used to warm Father Biname's feet on his own stomach. Father Franche and dad were like brothers, like father and son.

8

Never Come Back Home

Some new things were being introduced, called game laws. We needed licences for hunting and trapping in our own land. We were not as free as before. We were no longer able to hunt swans or musk ox, or they would give us a few years in jail. We had to get radio licences. Even boats had to be registered. It was crazy. We couldn't hunt cranes any more. But when we were hungry, sometimes we would hunt and to hell with the game warden. As far as I was concerned, a hungry mouth came first. I wouldn't allow my sick father to go hungry, nor my stepmother, nor my eight little brothers and sisters. The game laws couldn't feed us, they couldn't keep us alive. I only believed in my dad's laws, and the laws of nature. In the Far North, the strong survive and the lazy ones either starve or take handouts, though if a man is not a good hunter, he can help the women with chores, mostly cutting and hauling wood, and be looked after.

I didn't care about licences. I had been trapping without one since I was six. I was catching whisky-jacks then, and could already shoot with a gun.

I made a trip to Aklavik for some supplies. I had fourteen dogs pulling my sled. They weren't used to strangers and as we entered town, the dogs got excited and started chasing people. I could see guys running and stumbling along the wooden sidewalks and leaping into doorways. Allen Kris, the Jehovah's Witness, was one guy they chased. He was a real queer preacher who once, when I was just a small school boy, invited me over to his place. I didn't know any better.

I walked into his cabin and he told me to sit down. As I did, he locked his door on the inside with a padlock. Then he picked up a butcher knife and sat down in a chair facing me, starting to preach. This guy was mixed up and I was scared. He believed in reincarnation of the soul. And there was no hell but there were demons and demons were creatures of another dimension. And Jesus Christ was a witness of Jehovah and Jehovah was God. I had no intention of becoming a convert. I was satisfied with the Catholic Church. At least they don't lock you up to preach to you.

After four hours, I had had enough, so I lied. I lied and said I wanted to relieve myself outside. He unlocked the door and I ran all the way back to school. I had to get even with that guy for scaring me, so I let the dogs chase him. I dragged the sled anchor just enough so he wouldn't get caught. That was my own little joke. Those dogs wouldn't hurt anyone.

The run to Aklavik was good training for the Christmas dog race at Tuk. That was fun, too. A dog team can't eat too much before a long race, so the night before the big event, I went through town feeding every team a mixture of fish and castor oil. When we lined up on the start line the next day, the other teams were in bad shape and, of course, I won. I was travelling so fast the wind blew my cheeks out like balloons. And when I went over the finish line the hair on my head was frozen solid, sticking straight out back.

In the New Year, I fell for a cute girl named Elizabeth. I also fell for an Indian girl named Beatrice, and she was my first experience of kissing a girl on the lips. Kissing with Beatrice turned me on, but Elizabeth and I reached for the moon. She was a sweet little angel. We were both innocent and only thought of each other as friends, close friends. In the Eskimo tradition, love at the age of fourteen is natural and clean. We die early. We go by nature, not by the books. Girls have perfectly natural children at fourteen, some at twelve . . .

In 1953 Dad, who had been paralyzed for three years, had another stroke. This one almost killed him. Charlie went to town for help. I stayed with my stepmother till Charlie got back. Mike Zubko came out with Father Biname to our shack. Father Biname looked at my dad and said he'd better get him to hospital. So they took him to Tuk and put him on the boat for Aklavik which, at that time, was the site of the only hospital in the Delta.

I trapped for a while but we all missed dad, so we decided to move to Aklavik to be close to him. My stepmother, little Julia, William, Lawrence and Margarette—I led them all overland to Aklavik. Going over portages, I had to lift my 200-pound stepmother along with the rest. I was a man now. We moved into a shack in Aklavik. Dad had an operation and I was told he would be all right, but half of his body would be dead as before.

When dad was well enough, we went back out to our trapping camp near Tuk. I had to work like a man but I still played like a boy.

One day, Charlie was at the steering wheel of our scow. We were making something like fourteen knots. It was dark, and Charlie ran the scow up the back of Owen Allen's boat and pushed Red Andrew's scow under an overhanging tree. The tree hooked Old Red's overalls, lifted him up, and dumped him from the front of the boat into the back. Old Red was swearing like a Holy Roller.

On another day, I was out hunting geese and, on my way back, a big black bear jumped out in front of me. I had my shotgun and could have shot it easily but he got me by surprise. I dropped my load of geese and we both ran in different directions into the bush.

The first of July came and I was at the sports festival. Hugh Rodgers won the "long" race. I came in third in the 200-yard dash and got into the high jump, but it was stopped. Someone had stolen the bar.

Not long after dad returned home, he started his old drinking again, out of the big brew barrel. He was getting more and more cranky and fighting with my stepmother. One day I came home from my fish nets with Tommy. Dad was drunk. After a meal of frozen fish and whale oil and hot tea, I went to bed. I was asleep when I got hit with a broom handle. I got up and, without shoes or parka, I ran four miles to Old Abraham Teriglook's place. It was cold. Forty below. I only had socks on. I froze my ears a little but that was nothing.

Abe told me that when my parents sobered up, they would want me at home. I camped there and the old people adopted me for a while. Then I went back home. But nothing had changed. They were still my old drunken parents. In the meantime, Tommy had decided he'd had enough of that nonsense. He went out and got married.

The next spring I went trapping with Tommy and his wife and Charlie. We were on a big frozen lake. I was holding seven traps, an axe and an ice chisel when I went through the thin ice. I was in water up to my neck. The traps and axe sunk, but I floated. I started calling for help. Good old Tommy just fell over on his back laughing, and Charlie joined him. They were laughing so hard they were too weak to help me. I was in the hole up to my neck calling for help but all I got was a laugh. I was soaking wet. But it was worth it. We brought home some geese.

It's kind of out of season for geese in the spring but when a person doesn't get a weekly cheque from behind a desk, he only has one chance to think, and one chance to act.

That year the muskrat shooting was very poor and prices were even worse for fur. About four years earlier, we were getting three dollars for a muskrat fur. But now we were only getting ten to fifteen cents. It would sometimes take six months to get a thousand furs. Fifteen cents a fur comes to one hundred fifty dollars for half a year's work. Coloured fox pelts were only forty cents. You'd get seven dollars for a red fox and the top price for a white fox was twenty.

When summer came, Charlie went to work for the Mission and I stayed home. Soon after, we left for White Fish Station to hunt whales. I lost count of the whales we caught. There must have been more than sixty.

On the way home, we stopped to pick blueberries. For fun, we climbed some hills. I was fooling around with a friend, Stanley Kevik. We found a bear's hole. A good-sized one. I told Stanley to keep a watch out and I crawled into it. It was pitch black in there. I looked around but found nothing.

The next day I heard a commotion. Looking up, I could see these little girls and boys racing down the hill, all out of breath.

"What's the trouble?" I shouted.

"Bear!" one of the girls stuttered, flying by. "Up there on the hill!"

Just then I saw Stanley's wife and his two children coming towards me from the opposite direction. Stanley's wife said she had seen the bear earlier in the day while picking berries. Her little daughter had tugged at her dress, she said, and whispered, "Look, mommy, look at the big dog!"

"Some dog!" Stanley's wife said. "It stood about ten feet high. It was a big grizzly." And she added: "I thought to myself, 'they say if you don't stare at a bear and mind your own business, it'll leave you alone.' So I took my children, one in either hand, and led them away."

Hearing all of this, I figured I'd better go up that hill and have a look for myself. It was the dumbest thing I could have done.

I went up part way and this grizzly, a young one but big, suddenly stood up five feet from me. I picked up a rock, threw it and ran. The bear was right after me, behind me. I ran between small trees and willows, turning this way and that, like a young caribou singled out from the herd by a hunter, my heart pumping so hard I thought it would jump out of my breast. I tumbled most of the way down the hill and when I reached the bottom, the bear was gone.

By this time, some of the other men in the area had gone to get rifles. Mine was too far away to get. When a small group of them had formed at the bottom of the hill, they started up. I saw them disappearing over the top of the hill and then I heard a loud explosion. Six rifles being fired at once. I could see them waving then, and I ran up the hill. They pointed to some bushes where they said they had hit the bear. I took a long stick and went over and poked around. I found the bear. It was lying down and very still. I poked it and it jumped a little. Then Eliaz Kalinerk raised his rifle and fired one last shot that entered the bear's head. It slumped over dead. That day we had bear's meat. Three hundred of us feasted on it and it didn't last more than two meals.

That fall, my parents were still drinking and things were even worse. Then something happened which never should have. My stepmother got my dad worked up when they were both drunk. She took a broom to me, and dad took her side and drove me from home for good.

They told me never to come back and I left on foot with no food. I walked to Aklavik, nearly a hundred miles away. It took me three days, and I cried all the way. I know my dad loved me, but he had to back up my stepmother. I was hurt more than I had ever been before. I'd sooner have taken a whipping with a silver chain than be turned away by my dad.

When I got to Aklavik, I camped at John Waneltzie's place. Later I moved to John Alaska's. He's related to my dad. John's son, Moses, found me in the snow, stiff and cold. He thawed me out by the stove, and I started to feel strangely at home there. There was no one to scold me— for the first time in my life.

9

Going South

1955 came. I was seventeen years, five months and ten days old on New Year's Day. I was beginning a new life all on my own. I met some new girls, and I was free with them. The first one was from Fort McPherson. She was not much to look at, but she taught me the ropes. That was Bertha Peters. The next one was Emilie; then there was Florence; but it was Simonie who turned me into jelly.

I thought I was quite a man, when she said to me, "Don't ... please ... you'll make me pregnant ... "All that time, she hung on to me like I'd fly off somewhere. We were still there when her dad came in. He was a friend of *my* dad's, and he looked at me hard.

"Was she good?" he bellowed.

"Uh-yah."

"Then you should marry her!"

I shuddered at the thought, but all I said was I wasn't ready yet. Simonie touched my hand and gave me a look, as if to say, "Watch your step, boy." And I muttered some excuse like I had to chop some wood or feed my dogs or something and I left in a hurry. That was too close for me and I figured I had better watch out in the future.

I couldn't spend all my time with the girls. I had to earn a living. I flew by plane to the Reindeer Depot.

From there, Elija Sidney Itatchiak and I got a job together. We went by dog teams to the reindeer herd camp.
Elija was one year older than me, but full of spunk.

In the camp, we met Silas Kangeron and his family,
and Jimmy Komiak, the herd owner.

Elija Sidney and I stayed together, and we tried to
make our own mukluks. Elija's were good but mine
looked like two barges having a rough time in bad
weather. We made them of moose hide and canvas. In the
end, Mrs. Komiak and Mrs. Kangeron made us good
pairs of mukluks.

One day Elija and I had a wrestling match on the
lake. It lasted a long time. He was taller than me, but he
got tired, and I lifted him by his shoulders and hung him
by the back of his parka up a tree. He came down fast
when the branch broke.

There was a different kind of church there, a new
experience that got to me deeply. The Catholic Church
called them Holy Rollers, but from reading the Bible I
knew it was a true Christian kind of worship. Forty or
fifty grownup people all prayed together, all saying different prayers at the same time and speaking in different
tongues. It was an old form of gospel worship, I was told.
I was Catholic, but I knew the Catholic Church couldn't
help me, so I joined the group. It was great. I knew some
gospel songs from my childhood, and I sang them. I felt
the power of God come through in the church service. I
could feel something in the air, and in myself. It was
beyond my understanding, but it had to do with God.
There seemed to be a lightness in everyone in the room.

I met a man there who could do strange things with
his mind. One day, four of us were in a tent. My Bible
was in another tent, and this man said, "Tom is reading
your Bible." Not my brother, but another Tom. We
thought it was a joke, and asked him how he knew. He
said he could see him. Shortly afterwards Tom came in,

and we asked him what he had been doing. He said, "I was reading your Bible." I didn't understand how this man could know these things, and it impressed me deeply.

It was a lively church, too. You could smile, laugh, talk, be happy, cry, or do anything you wanted. I could see that people I knew who used to get drunk and fight with each other were changed because of these services. They had somehow developed a true belief in God.

Reindeer herding was fun but it had its problems.

Every afternoon we'd move the herd and check for strays. To do this, we had sleds pulled by deer trained to keep up with the lead reindeer in the herd and direct its course. I remember once taking five days to train a sled deer. When finally he had learned to follow the leader, I tied him up for the night, planning to harness him the next morning. At daylight, I went with a sled and harness and all I found was a pile of bones at the end of my rope. Some dogs had got loose in the night and eaten my sled deer. I had done five days of hard work for nothing. Well, the marrow was still there, so I ate it. Another time, I had a white sled deer which belonged to Wallace Luke's herd. I had to fight that deer to go four miles in four hours when we were leaving camp, but coming back it went like hell, doing four miles in about four minutes!

One night, I was in my snowhouse when I heard a wolf howl. My little herd dog looked frightened, though it seemed pretty quiet outside. Then suddenly, there was the sound of a stampede. The reindeer herd was racing away, and I hurried out into the cold. Seven deer were lying there dead. The wolves had got them. It had taken only a couple of minutes. By the time I had grabbed up my rifle, the wolves had scattered. I managed to wound one, but he got away with the rest.

There was a gas stove in the snowhouse and it over-heated one day and exploded on me. It burned my hood

off and some of my hair. From then on I used a tent and
a wood stove. The tent was colder than a snowhouse but
the wood stove was good for roasting meat.

When spring came, we moved the reindeer to the
coast. Elija and I took turns driving the herd. Abraham
Tajok was helping us. The does were dropping young
fawns on the way to Tuktoyaktuk so we took our time.
Thirty miles from Tuk, everyone but myself caught some
kind of 'flu and I was stuck with the herd for seven days.
In the spring the deer are really frisky. Even the young
ones. And when Silas Kangeron came to help me, I
dropped. That's how tired I was. When we got the herd to
Tuk, Elija quit and Sam Dick took his place. Sam was a
friendly little man, but his wife was friendly in another
way. I guessed she noticed that I had grown up. I stayed
with the herd until we got to Paulatuk, and then I quit
too.

Paulatuk was the place where I was born, and I left
my job because I met my sister Mary. I had not seen her
since I was three years old. When I met Mary, I didn't
recognize her, and she did not know me. But I saw this
big woman walking in front of me, and I asked her if she
knew Mary Kotokak. She said, "I'm Mary." I told her
who I was. Then I met my three nieces, Mona, Agnes and
Florence, and my brother-in-law, Edgar.

That summer I got a job on the Hudson's Bay Company freight ship, *Fort Hearne*. First mate Bill Sarks was
an old friend of my dad and we got along fine. Adam
Kinnerksanna, Andy Cackney, Sam Anerkinna, Bobbie
Gruben and Elija Sidney were deckhands with me. We
loaded at Tuk, then left for Coppermine in the East.
When we got there we had a dance, and I met a girl
named Alice. I went with her for a walk. She told me she
was getting married to a man called David. She was a
virgin and a sweet one, but she led me on when we were
alone. I later asked her why she gave herself to me and

not to her future husband. She told me I could have her any time, even after she was married.

From Coppermine, we headed across Coronation Gulf and through Dease Strait to Cambridge Bay on Victoria Island. It's a village with quite a few people. We unloaded part of our cargo and that night again, we danced. I ran into a woman called Agnes. She was married but she didn't tell me until after I took her down to the boat and we made love. Even after she told me she was married, we had nothing to hide. Everybody knew. To us, sex was good and love was clean, as long as you had a free innocent mind.

From Cambridge Bay, we sailed to Cash Haven and left the same day for Perry River. There I met a man who had gone through the ice on his trap line out in open water. He had frozen both feet. When the skin on his ankles and his feet went bad, he cut off his legs below the knees. When I saw him he was walking on his knees and still trapping.

From Perry River, we went to Spence Bay. I met a boy there who had experienced some hardships in life. One winter, his grandfather, mother, and three little brothers and sisters got caught in a big storm on a journey and were starving to death. The old man called to his grandson. He told him, "I am no more good and I am just a burden, a load for you, so if you want to live, kill me so I'll stop suffering and it will be easier for the rest of you." The old man made him put a gun to his head and pull the trigger. The young boy ... nine or ten years old then ... did it as a favour to his grandfather. After the old man died, the mother, to lighten their load, dug a hole in the snow and put caribou skins in it. Then she put her two little ones in the hole, covered them up to keep them warm, and journeyed off into the storm for home with her boy and baby. Sometime afterwards, she returned to the place with her boy to retrieve the two children, but they had frozen to death.

We made three boat trips east that summer, and I made twelve hundred dollars, giving most of it to my sister and her children. It's our way, that if you have more than someone else, you share it.

In the fall I went back reindeer herding for Bob Panaktak, but this time I stayed with the herd only for a few weeks. Then I went back to Tuk and got a job on the DEW Line.

DEW stood for Distant Early Warning. They were building these military stations at spots all along the Arctic Coast, the Canadians and Americans were. They said it was so they could see the Russians coming to attack the big cities down South. Some silly buggers used to stay up all night waiting for the war planes to come over. A station was even going up near the Eskimo village at Cape Parry. I wondered what old tattered Wallace Brown, the trapper, would have thought of that. He'd sure have looked funny coming out of nowhere in front of all those generals in their fancy get-ups and braided caps. Anyway, with fur prices lower than they'd ever been, at least the DEW Line helped to put a little bit of food in our stomachs. We couldn't complain about that.

There was a lot of construction in the Delta, too. The Canadian government men got the idea Aklavik was sinking to China or something. It was because every spring the Mackenzie would rise up a bit and flow into town. Some years, the water would be a foot deep in places. But mostly the town just got kind of muddy to walk around in. We didn't mind. Nobody seemed to mind, except the government people from the South. They didn't like to get their brand new bush boots dirty. So they were building a new town, thirty-five miles east across the Delta. Everybody called it E-3. But eventually the government men named the new town Inuvik. It means Place of Man.

Sometime after Christmas, I got to Cape Parry and

looked up my brother, Joe, and my sister, Bertha. I hadn't seen them in seventeen years. Joe had eleven children. I had earned a lot of money on the DEW Line. It was no good to me, so I gave three thousand dollars to Joe and spread another thousand among some other people. All I wanted was my freedom. I went out trapping white foxes and hunting caribou. I didn't have much luck though. The winter was poor, with storm after storm and lots of drifting snow and I couldn't get to my traplines. So in the spring I went to work for Northern Construction and only trapped in my spare time.

One day this government man came up to me and asked if I wanted to go South and take a six-week course in how to drive machines. He said the fur prices would never get better and I'd be wise to forget trapping altogether.

"The old days are gone," he told me. "The old days that your father knew are gone forever." I didn't want to believe him. But deep down I knew he was speaking the truth.

I remembered as a small boy in that first year at mission school seeing trappers in the spring coming into Aklavik with big smiles on their faces, their sleds heaped high with furs. You could hear them celebrating around their brew pots in the huts out behind the Anglican church. They were making a good living from trapping, then. The prices were good, the furs plentiful. But as the years passed, I saw their smiles turning to frowns. Fur prices were falling. By 1957, it was no longer possible to live by trapping alone. Half of the population of Aklavik was relying on government handouts. It was either that, or join the white construction gangs, or starve.

Part Three

They said I killed Charles Ratkovich

10

You Can Only Cross on the Green

I wanted to see the city that looked so beautiful in the pictures at mission school. The white man said I'd get better wages when I returned. So I went with a bunch from Aklavik and Tuk.

Over thirty of us piled aboard the big C-46 transport plane. We were laughing and joking as it roared down the runway and soared into the blue sky. Far beneath us, the muddy early-summer Delta gave way to blue-green forests and lakes. You could see the tiny, black shadow of the plane moving slowly across the landscape. But the beauty of it was lost on me. My stomach was turning. We were strapped into canvas-net seats running lengthwise along both sides of the plane. We had our Eskimo parkas on and the temperature felt like it was close to a hundred degrees. The constant bumping, the roar of the engines, my nervous anticipation of what lay ahead, all combined to make me airsick. Everyone was airsick. They gave us little brown, wax-paper bags to be sick in, but some of us couldn't wait for them to be handed out. And the putrid smell of vomit only made things worse.

Hours later. Dusk. Someone shouted that we were getting close to landing at Edmonton. I looked through the tiny window behind me, and I could see the lights, millions of beautiful lights. We were all looking out of the

71

plane at them. I had never seen anything like that in my life. We saw lots of cars and planes as we landed, and when we got off, we were put into taxis. I was still airsick as I took my first ride in a Yellow Cab. Riding into the city, our heads were turning right and left as huge, high buildings flashed by and people with fancy clothes strolled along wide concrete sidewalks.

We pulled up in front of a little rundown building. The sign said Alberta Hotel. We were taken inside and the manager took us up some stairs and gave us rooms. Two men to a room. Andy Cackney was put in with me. There was a big bed in the room, a sink, a place to stuff your clothes. That was about all. I couldn't figure out what the window was for. All you could see out of it was the blackened wall of the building next door. We were told to stay there until the federal government men came to get us. They were in Leduc, about twenty miles south of Edmonton, setting up our training camp. For twelve days, we were stranded in Edmonton. I had left my money in my baggage, and we couldn't get our baggage; none of us could, because the government men had it with them. They were arranging everything—everything but the bloody baggage. So I had no money for meals.

That first night we didn't leave the hotel at all. But the next morning early, a bunch of us went out to see what was going on. We didn't go far—just two or three blocks, then we turned around and came back.

Soon though, curiosity won out. Our initial fear drained away, and our walks became daily adventures. We spent hours exploring the busy streets, looking through windows at fancy shops as people in big-city costumes rushed around us and in and out of towering buildings that made everybody look tiny.

There was so much to learn. First, we had to learn how to keep out of the way of all those honking cars. We just crossed the streets anywhere, and the policemen stopped us. They called it jaywalking. Most of them were polite. But some must have mistaken us for the Indians who drank around our hotel, because they would get rough. The good policemen told us what to do. They told us to cross only where streets come together, where the lights change colours. They showed us how the traffic lights work, so we wouldn't cross among the cars. "You can cross on the green," one said. But even after being told, we didn't do too well. We'd still end up crossing right among the cars.

We didn't know how to use sidewalks either. When the whole bunch of us were out walking, we'd take up the entire sidewalk. Pretty soon we learned to use only one half of it, so other people could get by without having to step out into the line of cars.

We were helped out by the people we met outside of the hotel. I know now they were Skid Row bums, but they were the only ones who would talk to us. We didn't know any women, so they took us to some. It turned out they wanted money. They were selling themselves. They said: "You want sex? Gimmie ten dollars."

Up North, it's just natural, but down South, you had to buy it. I didn't have any money so I spent most of the time alone in my room.

I wondered how I was supposed to get food in that place. There was an eating room downstairs but you needed money. It was sure not like where we had come from. Up North, we could get seals, polar bears, and caribou to eat. We could get them right out of the country. In that hotel, you couldn't get anything unless you paid for it. Well, at least I could get water out of that rusty sink and I could get a wash once in a while. There was even a place for taking a leak. It was a room just down the hall that had a wash tub. Up in the North, we used to take leaks outside or else in an empty butter can. When I first got to that hotel, I couldn't find the toilet, so

I used the garbage bucket in my room.

The first toilet we ever used was on the plane coming down. We couldn't find anything to wipe ourselves with. Some paper was there, I guess but we couldn't see it. When we got to the hotel, somebody found the toilet and told me where it was. It had paper. But we soon ran out. We didn't know what to do then, so we used any kind of paper or tore up the covers from the beds. The toilet was soon plugged up and was splashing all over.

At night, the people we had met changed. During the day they were all right, but at night they all seemed to go wild. There were drunks fighting all over the place, so I would go to my room early and get out of their way. I didn't know what to do. I didn't know about movie theatres or stuff like that then, and I couldn't have paid for them anyway.

About the third day we were there, we saw a gang fight out back of the big fancy hotel, a few blocks away from our hotel. George Tardiff, Albert Bernhardt, Guy Omilgoitok, Andy and myself. Grown boys were beating up little ones. All at once the police came. Some of the boys got caught, and some got away in cars. One of the cars was completely loaded down, with boys riding on the top and hanging out the sides. All kinds of fancy women from the hotel were watching, too. We didn't understand, but we didn't like what we saw. It made us feel sick and trapped.

All of a sudden Albert said, "You old enough to go to the liquor store?"

Well, I wasn't. I wasn't quite twenty. But I said, "Let's get some beer." Albert changed that to whisky.

Guy said, "Let's get some whores."

I didn't have any money. I hadn't even eaten yet. But Albert had money so I said, "Hell, let's try it."

We found two women. It was the first time I ever saw two women take on six guys at once, and make a lot of money for it in less than an hour. It was quite a surprise. These nice-looking women had less morality than the most primitive people you could ever find.

The more I drank, the freer I felt. I started acting like the people on the street. Late that night, we got back to the hotel feeling pretty high. I remember waking up after passing out. I had to go to the toilet. I got to my feet and walked down the hall and when I opened the washroom door and looked in, there was Guy Omilgoitok asleep in the bath tub. It was full of puke and water. I used the washroom anyway but the smell of that puke got me and, as I started to weave back to my room, I got sick myself. I let go and the liquor came splashing out all over the floor. It was a real mess. But that's the way things were in that part of town.

After that party, I started to drink a lot. I'd hook up with guys I'd meet in different hotels, guys from the DEW Line stations up North, and I'd end up drinking with them. It went on day after day. One time I got really drunk, and my cousin Danny Smith and another Eskimo had to carry me out of a hotel bar. They had to take me out the back way because the police were coming in the front.

The next day, Andy took me to a café and we had a meal. It was the Coffee Cup on 96th Street. God, what a sight! People were fighting at the door. But it was good to get some food in me.

Some of the boys got something new, VD, and most of us picked up new habits. We thought they were white man's ways. I slicked my hair down with Noxzema Face Cream. I brushed my teeth with shaving lather. I used to wash my face with mouthwash. I couldn't read labels at all, and I ended up chewing laxatives like candy.

My people in the North were struggling with the same problems. Southern ways were spreading into the Arctic, and my people knew nothing of these new habits and customs, and couldn't grasp many simple things that the white man had accepted for decades. When Kotex napkins were first sold to the Eskimo people, the girls used them as knee pads and ear muffs, till they got wise. And when contraceptives first came to Aklavik, we didn't know what they were. We thought they were balloons, and we blew them up all over town. A friend of mine got a hospital bill, and he tried to cash it at the Hudson's Bay store. An Eskimo woman at Tuk made a doll to sell to the Department of Northern Affairs, but she made it too male, with a penis, and they wouldn't accept it.

I'll never forget the time I stopped my dog team in front of the hotel at Aklavik, and got a ticket for illegal parking. And then there was the Eskimo at Tuk, who was speeding along with his dog team, and he collided with an airplane. He didn't know about airplanes. A friend of mine was once charged with dangerous driving. He hit an RCMP boat with his kayak. He didn't see it coming—he was blind in one eye. There is still a sign on the road along the DEW Line at Tuk. It says, "Caution, Eskimo Crossing, Drive Slowly."

One afternoon, we came back to the hotel after a night and morning of drinking. About six of us. We were told that the government men had come to collect the rest of our bunch. They had gone to Leduc. We didn't know what to do. Some of the boys made up their minds to buy a car. I don't know how we put together the money but the next day we went out and bought one. A beat-up thing. I don't remember the make. But I'm sure it didn't have brakes. Danny slid behind the wheel and we scraped curbs all the way out of Edmonton. The police couldn't have caught us if they'd tried. Boy! What a wild ride! Some of us were pretty scared. We thought that maybe we were going to hit something. But Danny turned out to be not a bad driver, aside from scraping a few curbs. I don't know how we found our way to Leduc. But we did.

The white news reporters were waiting for us after we got settled. They said we were the first Eskimos to come South under a Canadian Government Manpower Training Program. They didn't know how sick we were. We were hung over and the summer heat was terrible. It was fifty above on the Arctic Coast and over eighty degrees in Leduc. We had no thought in the world but to get out of that heat, and go home. Sometime later, we saw the newspapers, and my picture was all over Page One. I was smiling in the picture, but at the time I didn't feel like smiling. I had a real bad headache, and the reporters were asking all these questions. Later that day, I collapsed. When I came around, I tried aspirin, but it was no good. Then I tried beer. I drank some whisky, then a whole bottle of Lemon Hart rum. It didn't make me feel better. It made me feel weaker. I was a little drunk, and I went to see our instructor. He said I had pneumonia.

Funny how a man can stand seventy or eighty below zero weather, and can catch this kind of sickness under a hot sun. From the pneumonia and heat shock, I almost died. I don't know how I got the few miles to the Charles Camsell Hospital in Manning. For a while I was unconscious in an oxygen tent, and when I came to, I saw that nearly everybody from our group was in there with me. I read in a medical book that alcohol slows your body's blood pressure down, and gives you resistance to heat. So when I got out of hospital, I drank beer every day, and more and more of it.

Back in Leduc, our training started. Mechanical work was not too difficult, but electrical servicing and repairs were problems for me. I never *did* like electric shocks. Eventually though, I learned to operate and service diesel power plants, and I got high marks on grader operating.

Most of us caught on pretty quickly because we had seen the same type of graders used up on the DEW Line. Once in a while, we'd drive them just to see how they worked.

I'll never forget my first day driving a truck on the course. I was driving the whole bunch out to the training field and I came to a railway crossing. I didn't know much about railroad tracks. But someone told me you're supposed to stop and look and listen when you come to them. Well, I braked all right, but the truck didn't stop skidding until it was right on top of the tracks. You should have seen the boys scramble! A train was coming and I had stalled the engine. Somehow I managed to get it going again before the train came. That was enough for me. The next time I came to those tracks, I didn't bother stopping. I drove over them as fast as I could.

That was my formal education. I don't remember much of it. I was too busy getting sick and drunk.

We were bunked in private homes. After the course each night, we'd head for the bar, and end up going home kind of high. I was staying with Wolkie, Albert Bernhardt and one of the Banks Island boys. Albert was the worst. He was always coming home drunk. I tried to straighten him out once. I went out back of the house and picked up some shit from the toilet and stuffed it between his bed sheets. Albert came home that night, drunk as usual, and went right to bed with his clothes on. He tossed and turned in his sleep a lot. And when he woke up in the morning he looked at himself. He was covered from head to toe. He couldn't figure out how he could get so dirty without pulling his pants down. It seemed that nothing would work with Albert. He carried right on with his drinking.

Me too. I began drinking *before* as well as *after* school. It seemed to me the thing to do. I thought all white men must do it, because all of the ones I saw did.

In our spare time, we would take trips to Edmonton. We bought suits of clothing at the Hudson's Bay Company department store with the money we got from the government. And we were so dumb, we wore them over our pajamas. I tried walking in cowboy boots, but I couldn't stand in them, much less walk. I couldn't walk in Oxfords, either, without my feet bleeding.

My introduction to civilization was Skid Row. I met the pimps and prostitutes. I met the bums, bootleggers and muggers. I met the street fighters and their broads, dope addicts and pushers and hustlers.

We were like children down there. Lost. I got beaten and robbed of a ninety-five-dollar Polaroid camera and almost two hundred dollars. There was a Bible, a new one with my name in it, and they took that, too. Two women robbed Wolkie of four hundred dollars. Lots of us were robbed—many times. I would give money to old people on the street. They looked sick and hungry, and our religious training and Eskimo way of life taught us never to leave anybody hungry or cold, if we could help them in any way.

I met a French-Canadian girl in Leduc. She was very nice, but when she put me down, I went with any girl in the street. I was thinking of marriage to a girl back home but while I was away taking the course, she married someone else, one of my cousins. I got the news in a letter from home. This hurt me, so I went to Edmonton and got myself a twenty-dollar-a-night girl. Women in Edmonton were selling sex like merchandise. One day in a Leduc bar I ran into a different kind of thing. This guy was asking me to pay him five dollars so he could suck me off. I asked him what he meant. I had never heard of such a stupid thing. I got the bartender to chase him off.

I was glad when August came. Six of us went home. And I got the surprise of my life.

11

Downtown, Dead Drunk

Before the course, I was making as much as twelve hundred dollars a month in some jobs. Now I was only able to make two hundred dollars a month, plus room and board, working sixteen hours a day in the jobs the government found me. I worked seven days a week, sometimes without sleep. During the course, I lost the girl I wanted to marry. Now this.

My first job after returning North was at a DEW Line site. Construction was finished by then. For miles across the barren Arctic plain, you could see the huge snow house-shaped buildings in which they housed the electronic eyes that constantly scanned the sky. The soldiers worked in darkened rooms inside long, low slender buildings. Day and night, they kept their eyes glued to screens, watching for strange "blips", and outside the North Wind noisily tried with all of its might to bury the Southern invaders in a sea of swirling snow. My job was outside, hauling water with a truck. It was sixty below one day, and the foreman turned the water hose on me. I quit. I couldn't work with that man. I left there and went trapping.

Construction of the new town of Inuvik was continuing. By 1959, it was the place to go when you wanted a drink. On the eastern end of town, fancy homes were going up for the white government people and construction chiefs who were making Inuvik the new administrative centre in the Western Arctic. They were heated with nice warm air piped in from a central heating plant. So were the new Roman Catholic and Anglican schools. Aklavik was becoming a ghost town. Everything was being moved over. Half of the native families I had known in Aklavik were living now in Inuvik. They were on the western end of the town. Teepee Town we called it— everybody called it—because there weren't any houses at the west end. Just tents and shacks made with packing cases, odd boards and sacking. Wood stoves kept them snug and warm. And at night the homebrew flowed.

It was there that I got the news that I was the father of a boy. The name of the mother is Gabriel Kalousak. I promised her something I never promised to any other girl in my life, and I'll never break that secret promise. I loved her a lot, but liquor took her away from me. She went off with a blue-eyed blonde Norwegian guy. She said if I loved her, I wouldn't stop her. I didn't even try to get her back. My uncle and auntie from a reindeer station adopted my son. His name is Ronnie. I used to go and visit him when he was little. The last time I saw him, he was five.

Late in the spring, I worked for Northern Arctic National Resources, a federal government company, for a dollar-seventy-five an hour. I worked for the company for five months, but I was drinking heavily now and had spent some time in jail.

In 1960, I even helped to build the RCMP jail cells at Inuvik. They were built at about the same time the liquor store opened. It was as if they were getting ready for a big commercial enterprise. There were hardly any prisoners before the store but the day it opened, the six cells, the jail block floor, the hallway—all were littered with drunks —more than fifty of them. I saw a whole family locked up that night. Even the judge had to be led home. It was funny to see the entire population of Inuvik, at least the entire population of the west end, lining up to buy liquor. But that's what it looked like on that historic day. Almost every night after that, the jail would be full. I remember seventeen of us Eskimos were once picked up for being drunk. We were only too happy to co-operate with the police. We pleaded guilty because everyone else did. Some of my people would get drunk just to see what it was like in jail. Now when I think of how we all used to plead guilty, I want to laugh. I know now that there are lawyers, people trained to protect innocent people. Some of those lawyers are even smarter than policemen.

That year I got my first criminal record. I had some rum and I gave a drink to a man I knew as Eli Norbert. He got drunk and got his leg broken in a fight. I had never heard of a Treaty Indian, but Eli was one. The government convicted me of supplying him with liquor. That summer I also caught a bad case of VD. It was all over the North.

I journeyed to Aklavik. There I met up with a girl named Pauline. I really fell for her. We were together for five months and I wanted to marry her, but the Catholic Church wouldn't allow it because she was my half-cousin, and she was Anglican. They wouldn't let us intermarry, something the Eskimos had been doing for years.

One night, when I was at Tuk in 1962, I thought I saw two shadows making motions for me to follow. I was staying with my sister, Mary, and my four nieces. I asked them if they could see these two things calling me. I had a strange feeling and I told Mary, "Dad is calling. Something is wrong with him."

I took a snowmobile to Inuvik and found that my father had died of a heart attack.

I couldn't sleep for three nights after his burial. Finally, I took two bottles of rum and knocked myself out.

I kicked around Inuvik for a while but it got me into

more trouble. Old L. F. Semmler, Millionaire Semmler we called him now, had a brand new hotel in Inuvik called the Mackenzie Inn. He had a bar in there where we did a lot of our drinking. One night after downing quite a few I went into Stan Peffer's Café to buy some supper. The café was empty, but somebody had left the door open. As I entered, the door slammed behind me and I was locked in until morning. The police came and I was charged with breaking and entering with intent to steal. My only intention was to get out of there. They didn't believe me, and I was sentenced to three months in jail.

My dad's death, my new criminal record, the VD, and my trouble with girls made me head back to my home village of Paulatuk.

In late fall, I went out to my trapline and made a mistake on the open ice. I forgot to watch the wind shifting from northeast to southwest, and I found myself stranded on an ice floe in a storm. I had thirteen dogs and only a few fish. It was hard to see in the storm and I made a snow house and waited. The first night was not bad. I managed to catch two seals and feed the dogs, but two weeks later I was still out there. One night the wind was bad and I lost four dogs. When I awakened, they were frozen to the ice. By the time the fourth week arrived, I was hungry and my dogs were starving. Two more dogs froze on the ice and I cut them up and fed them to the remaining dogs, and ate some myself. It was like bear meat.

I now had seven dogs left. On the thirty-first day, the wind took me somewhere close to Pearce Point. But the weather was still bad and I couldn't tell just how close to shore we came. My blankets were frozen stiff. I had a stove with one gallon of coal oil. One of the dogs was frozen on one side, and the hair came off. He was one that had worked especially hard to help me and I didn't have the heart to shoot him. I made a snow house for him and left him some scrap bones.

That day I almost gave up hope. I was very tired and I thought if I fall asleep, I'm done. I remember my dad telling me never to give up. If you have a will, you have hope.

Finally, the storm let up a little. Thirty miles away I could see the Paulatuk Hills. My heart leapt. I helped my six dogs to pull the sled, and made it there in nine hours. I had a ten dollar Timex wristwatch from the Hudson's Bay Company, and I used it as a compass. No one was around in Paulatuk. There was an old oil stove in the Mission church. I entered and lit it. The old Father won't mind, I thought. I put my dogs inside the covered porch and found some cornmeal and seal oil, and fed them and myself. I also found some coffee and some of Father's wine. I thawed it out, drank only one cup, and put the bottle back.

The next day I continued my journey, stopping at Bennett Point to camp. It was a beautiful moonlit night. The following morning I was on my way again, and that night I camped at Letty Harbour. The next day I got a few miles from Cape Parry, and my dogs gave up. I was helping them but they were too tired, so I tied them up. I had a little piece of fish, and I cut it up and gave it to them.

It was blowing hard, and I made a little snow house. It was just big enough so that I could sit in it and kneel down. For the first time I prayed to God to help me make it home.

The wind dropped. I picked up my rifle and left the dogs. I figured I would get them later, but now they needed rest. I was weak, and three miles of walking seemed like many more, and it took me about six hours. My journey home had taken me one month and five days. Most of this time my people thought I was fishing. On the day I arrived home a plane was going out to look for me.

I was quite a sight, my parka and blankets were stiff with ice, and it took nearly half an hour by the stove to thaw my parka out so I could get it off.

I was lucky.

I have known many people who never came back. I recall one hunter who went out looking for caribou, and his body was never found. We think he must have rolled himself up in a raw caribou skin. If you wrap the skin around you, even in twenty-below weather, you are stuck in there for good, to starve. The skin freezes hard and you can't get out.

There are all kinds of ways of dying out there. Some people get tired, and go to sleep, and never wake up. Freezing makes you sleepy. There is loss of pain when your brain starts to freeze. I have felt that way more than once.

1963 came. I went to work on the sea lift which supplied the DEW Line. They sent me to Cape Dyer in the forest on the east coast of Baffin Island. I worked there for two hundred dollars a month, until one day I met a white man who acted like a woman. He asked me to his room. There he took off all his clothes, and rubbed his legs against my knees. He was six-foot-three, about 240 pounds of rippling muscles, and it scared the hell out of me. I took off when he asked me to jam it up his ass. I didn't want to stick around that guy so I got myself fired by getting drunk.

That same week I was hired at Foxe Basin as an assistant night shift foreman on the airlift. I moved on to Tuk after a while, and it was there that my drinking went right out of control.

The police soon got sick of me. I was picked up for being drunk twenty-three times in nine months. When I think of the fines I paid, I only hope the money was used to help poor people somewhere. I was accused under the law for other things, but I never did understand the charges. I would always plead guilty because the police told me it would make things easier for me.

In the winter of 1964-65, I was sent to an alcoholic rehabilitation centre. It is in Belmont, Alberta, near Edmonton. I was twenty-seven. And they said I was ruining my health and decreasing my fortune and property by drinking. I was at the alcoholic centre for four months. By the time I got out, I had learned some things about alcohol, and what it can do to you. I moved to a halfway house in Edmonton with some other boys. One of them was Cliff W. We stayed sober for about two weeks, then the big city got to us. We went uptown to look around. I took one drink, and then another, and ended up stitting in a bar until midnight. I was pretty high when I got back to the halfway house. I knocked on the door too hard. It was a big glass one, and the glass came down on me. I remember Duke Parrish, who ran the house, telling me to come back when I was sober.

I went back downtown and got dead drunk and wound up with a cute-looking white girl. She asked me if I wanted to have some fun. I said sure, and we went up to her room at the hotel. We were both naked in bed when three guys busted in. They were strong-arm guys. I didn't know it, but she was their bait and I was the fish. I took a beating I'll never forget. They used a table leg on me. I was covered in blood, but they couldn't finish me and eventually they let me go with the warning that if I went to the police they'd charge me with rape. They said the girl was under-age, though she had told me she was eighteen. I walked up the road. Suddenly everything went dark, even the streetlights, and I didn't know anything for a long time. Five or six days later, I came to in the Charles Camsell Hospital. I felt the pain in my head for a moment. I screamed with the pain and blacked out again. I had spinal bleeding and a bad concussion of the brain. I kept losing my mind for two months. After that my mind was not too good any more. And I had trouble remembering people I knew.

From the Charles Camsell, I was sent to the Alberta Hospital (Oliver). I call it the nut house because there were a bunch of people there who were crazy. I was in for three weeks. They made me sit on the side of the bed and they placed a whole row of bottles in front of me. Bottles partly filled with different kinds of liquor. They hooked some kind of an electrical gadget to my back and they said, "Go ahead, help yourself, Tony, anything you want. What you think is best for you."

I picked up the rum, took a big slug right out of it. I just about went out of my mind with the pain. I could hear a voice behind me saying, "Leave that stuff alone in future, Tony, or you will feel the pain again."

I picked up some beer, and it was the same all over again. I could hear the doctor's voice, but I couldn't see him.

I went back to Inuvik. It was the fall of 1965. That little bit of treatment stuck in my mind. I managed to stay sober for a year. But my mind was confused, and I could only hold a job for a few weeks at a time.

I have always believed in spirits, good or bad.

When I was two years old, I would see this old woman. No one else could see her. She was white-haired and had large eyes like my sister's. I was not afraid of her.

At Inuvik, I saw this same old woman in a little house where I was visiting with my auntie and my cousins.

We were having a quiet party. There was a knock on the door. We answered it but no one was there. The same thing happened a second time. The third time we heard knocking, I went to the door alone.

I saw the face I had seen when I was a small boy.

The footfalls were clear, the breath could be heard. Her face was old, her hair white, her eyes were large like my sister's. My cousins could hear the noise but could not see the figure. My auntie could, and she fainted. The old lady was dressed in a long caribou parka of the kind Alaskan women used to wear. There was wolf fur around her hood.

She told me not to be afraid, and she said she watches me always. "I'm your relation," she said. Ilugivialukinma. "I am your real relation." Erksinngerrin. "Do not be afraid." Monargemubmiyupkin. "I am watching you." Ataramik.

After saying that, she vanished. My auntie told me it was my father's mother. She knew her face. My grandmother, Mary Khingaogak. She died many years before I was born.

Another time, at another house, I saw something on the floor that no one else could see. This thing came out of the stove fire and it looked like a red eagle. It scratched the floor hard, and only I could hear it. When its head turned, it changed from an eagle to a fox. It looked like an ancient gargoyle from an Old Country myth. I was afraid I was going insane, so I went to a priest and told him of what I saw.

He told me that the spirit world exists. And this disturbed me even more.

Once at Letty Harbour, close to Paulatuk, before I first went South, a bunch of us were camped beside an old storehouse for the night. The dogs got restless. Then we heard someone in there throwing empty cans around and banging on things. Joe Roy went to look, but it was dark and he couldn't see. The next morning, we checked again. There was no one in the house. There were no cans, no nothing. Not even tracks leading away in the snow.

A ghost even haunted the DEW Line site at Pearce Point. A girl I knew died from food poisoning, and her ghost could be seen and heard.

When you are all alone, in a dark room with no sound to disturb your mind and concentration, light two candles, one on each side of you. Then sit or kneel between the candles. Close your eyes and concentrate on the sound of the flames. If the room is not disturbed by natural sounds, you will hear the flames talk to each other. They will inspire you in a language you have never heard before. You will understand what you are told, but you will not remember the language. You will come out with wise decisions to plan your life.

Moving between Inuvik and Tuk, I worked for the Northern Transportation Company, Northern Arctic National Resources, Ray Geophysical, then N.A.N.R. again. Then the Fred Norris Company. Finally, in the fall, I went back to work for Canadian National Telecommunications, running power plants and a repeater station on the telephone line at Thunder Bay.

For three months I worked out of a trailer. I did a carving of an Eskimo sitting with a drum, and a man dancing in front of him. Their faces were expressionless. I couldn't make them look happy because I wasn't happy myself. The man who bought the carving did not understand how I felt in isolation. His idea of art was to see figures with happy faces. To me, beauty in that instance was reflected in the imperfect figures showing the real feelings of hardship I was undergoing at the time.

One morning, I woke up in the trailer feeling weak. Blood was coming from my nose and mouth. I was throwing up and could hardly manage to crawl outside. Carbon monoxide poisoning. The gas had escaped from the power plants. I got scared and phoned the station at Inuvik, ninety miles away.

When I got to the hospital at Inuvik, I was told I didn't have an appointment and would have to come back. So I went uptown and got drunk. I was bushed and sick. I lost my job and ended up in the hole to income tax for one hundred and thirty-seven dollars. I got no isolation pay, no holiday pay, and no compensation for sickness. The C.N.T. found beer in the trailer and they blamed that, and not carbon monoxide poisoning, for my problems.

About then somebody told me I had two children at Foxe Basin, another two at Tuk, and one at Reindeer Depot. Two more girls had me marked, too, so in May 1967, when I got my chance, I moved South again. A policeman told me a man of my knowledge could do well down there.

I drank my way to Peace River. There I met a bunch of guys in a bar who suggested we hire a cab to take us to Edmonton. When we got to Edmonton, they threw open the back doors of the cab at a stop light and ran for it. I was stuck with the fare.

I got clubbed in a back alley and landed in the Charles Camsell again. Back in Edmonton, four times in one week I got picked up for being drunk.

12

Anybody's Riverbank Pal

I wandered from one hotel to another, looking for a drink, sleeping where I could. Most nights it was a little burnt-up shack we called the Sugar Shack. I went there the first time with an Indian girl I met outside the liquor store on 97th Street. She was with the other prostitutes, and winos, waiting for the doors of the liquor store to open at ten o'clock. Her name was Riverbank Mary. Everybody was fucking her down by the riverbank.

"All you need is a bottle of wine," they told me.

I bought one and I could see her licking her lips, so I said, "Sure, let's go!"

We went, right in broad daylight, down behind the big hotel. We were making love on the open grass. Drinking at the same time. And a policeman—he wasn't a real constable, more like a watchman—came up behind us. He told us we'd better get up and move out of there.

"Everybody's looking at you," he said.

That made me look up. I could see their faces then, in the windows of the huge brown castle-like structure, hotel people, dozens of them, staring down at us. They were looking at me ramming Mary. We got up fast and ran and hid in the bushes.

Later, Mary took me down to the Saskatchewan River. Arm in arm we went down to the riverbank. We made love again. Then we just lay back and had a little drink and looked at the sky. I asked her how many boy-friends she had around that place. She gave me a bunch of names. Then she snuggled up to me and said, "I'll tell you the truth. I'm anybody's riverbank pal."

Then she asked me how many girlfriends *I* had. I started counting, but when I ran out of fingers, I stopped. She was asleep by then, anyway.

Some hours later, we woke up. The sun was dipping behind the big buildings in the distance and the air was chilled by the water from the river. We picked ourselves up and walked back to the liquor store to get some more wine.

Later, Mary took me to the Sugar Shack where I spent a lot of nights after that. The shack was just down the street from the seven-million-dollar CN building. The trains owned by the rich Canadian National Railway went right past it. Nobody was there when we went in. We lay down and drank some more, and then we fell asleep making love. When morning came and I opened my eyes—Holy Smoke—I could see eight, maybe ten, bums all passed out and lying around in the ashes. You couldn't tell who was white and who was Indian. Every-body was black from lying in the ashes. Mary and me too. I woke her up.

"We've gotta get out of here," I said.

But it was too late. They were already stirring. Two of them were grumbling and one said to the other, "If you can't hustle, you won't bum with me anymore." We all ended up pooling our money to get some wine.

We spent a lot of time together—Mary and me. She was a nice girl. But just like any Eskimo who came South, she couldn't adjust to the new society. So she turned to drink to forget she was a rejected person. She had no chance to do anything else.

I had other girls, of course. One whose name I can't mention now, I'll just call her Kathie, was with me when I

ended up at a house party one night on the east side of
Skid Row. There was a real, mixed-up bunch at the party.
They were real tough people. A friend told me not to stay,
to get out of there before I got into trouble. So I left. But
Kathie stayed behind. That night I slept close to the railroad tracks, in the grass. It was raining a little bit, but I
pulled my coat over me and managed to stay warm. The
liquor helped. In the morning, I walked uptown and a
policeman came up to me.

"Were you with that girl last night?"

"Yah."

"Where did you leave her?"

I pointed in the direction of the house.

"Down there."

"Inside or outside?"

"Inside. Downstairs."

The policeman told me her body had been found
outside the house. She had been strangled. I don't know
who did it. She was a nice girl, a good friendly person,
even though she was on Skid Row.

Some of the people were real bad. I remember an
Indian and a white girl approached me on the street near
the liquor store.

"Come on with us," the Indian said. "We'll show you
a bottle of wine." He told me to stand out front of the
liquor store. He told me, "When you see someone come
out, start talking to him. Walk with him and we'll follow
you."

I did this with the first guy I saw coming through the
door. I didn't think anything bad would happen. But
when we had walked a while and got to a section of the
street where nobody was around, the Indian and the
white girl showed up behind us.

Bang! They grabbed the guy and shoved him against
a building and punched him and took the bottle that he
had bought at the liquor store. They even went through

his pockets.

"Come on. Let's go," they said finally. I took a quick look at the guy to see if he was okay, before running off with them. I was learning the dirty tricks of Skid Row.

I tried to slow down, tried to slow my drinking down, so I could get a job and pick myself up. But I couldn't get one. I turned to the welfare people. They would give me a bed, ten at night till eight in the morning, then kick me out for the day no matter what kind of weather. I could stand the cold, but the rain would make me awfully sick.

I used to wake up with heavy hangovers, and one morning I couldn't talk straight without stuttering. After that, I drank more and when I fell asleep my dreams were of falling and my heart beat wildly. When I woke up, I saw faces coming out of the wall, staring at me. My mind was numb and I began to say things that made no sense. Once I saw a man coming up to me, but he disappeared when I touched him. No one else had even seen him.

Down at the Sugar Shack, there was a gang of Indians and whites, drinkers like me. They asked me to join them. They were breaking into garages and stealing stuff and selling it. Well, it was a way to buy booze. I came close to going to jail one night. All of us were sitting in the grass behind the York Hotel down by the railway tracks. We were drinking that stuff you use in making pies—extract. Suddenly two policemen appeared. I had a great big 24-inch pipe wrench sticking out of my back pocket. The younger one spotted it. He wanted to know what I was doing with that. I told him I had found it.

Just then the bottle of extract caught the eye of the other policeman. One of the guys was trying to hide it.

"What's this?" the policeman said, reaching down to pick it up. The other one forgot about the pipe wrench and came over to join his partner.

"What do you do with it?" the young policeman asked, taking the bottle in his hand to read the label. We told him we drank it.

The policemen just stared at us for a long time and then the younger one said,

"You guys—you're gonna die, you know."

He gave us back the bottle and they walked away, nodding their heads and talking quietly to each other. They never did take a close look at the pipe wrench. It was my lucky day.

I ended up testing a lot of different things instead of waiting for another day. Like rubbing alcohol. You pour water into a bottle till it is about two-thirds full. Then you pour in enough of that pure alcohol until it turns white inside. Then you drink it. I first drank rubbing alcohol with a bunch of old army guys. They were passing this bottle around. I looked at it and it was marked poison, with a skull on it. But, boy, they were drinking a lot of it and when nobody died for an hour or so, I tried a bit myself. I got feeling pretty high.

On Sundays, when the liquor store was closed, I'd sometimes get rubbing alcohol from the bootlegger's. When he ran out of liquor, he'd sell that. He even used to put it in some of the wine he sold.

It sure wasn't great to wake up with a swollen head, sick and hungry, right in the middle of the big city, but the people I met were all like me, and the others were too smart for me. I couldn't talk to them.

Skid Row alcoholics seem to find very strange spots to drink—back alleys, a riverbank, a hotel washroom. A favourite with us was spiking coffee in dingy little back rooms. We also filled up Coke bottles and guzzled from them in cafés. I even learned how to pick up cigarette butts like a genuine bum.

Thanksgiving Day in Edmonton. To me it was like any other day. Two Indians were after me for drinks and I got a bloody nose and a black eye from them. I went to a hotel to see if I could bum a meal but the same two boys were there so I took off with an old Indian friend. He had a dollar so he got a bottle of rubbing alcohol. I had forty cents, and with it I got a bottle of shaving lotion.

He said he knew where we could get something special to eat. He took me uptown to a rich district. There was a bunch of fancy houses and we went along this little road that ran behind them. I watched my friend picking into the garbage cans. He came up with some turkey bones with some meat on them. He put them in a brown paper bag and went on. Out of other garbage cans he got some rotten apples and old dried bread. He put these in the bag too. He got quite a bit of stuff. We walked down to the river and he said, "Let's celebrate Thanksgiving Day." So we did. We had our Thanksgiving dinner right there beside the Saskatchewan River. Even something to drink. It didn't taste too good but at least it filled our stomachs and helped us fight the dampness of the night.

Sometimes I would find a pair of shoes or some clothing better than the ones I had on, and I'd go into a back alley or a gas station washroom for a quick change. I remember one day spotting a Skid Row friend who usually wore rags. He was dressed to the hilt in a conservative suit. He had swiped it from an unlocked hotel room. On another occasion, I got some good clothes from the Sally Ann, all brand new. I passed out on the riverbank and when I woke up I only had my socks, pants and T-shirt left. Someone had taken my jacket, shirt, shoes and wallet. One time a man came up to the room I was staying in. He showed me some gold watches and talked me into buying one. I found out later it had no motor, just a block. Tricks like that have been played on me many times.

You can never tell who you'll meet on Skid Row, or what they're up to. They see a simple Eskimo who knows nothing of frame-up artists, bookies, loan sharks, crooked

ticket-sellers, bootleggers, pimps, prostitutes, queers, muggers, and they prey on you. Like the two boys I came
across. They seemed nice enough and acted real friendly,
but all the time they were after the money they knew I had
on me. They came up behind and started beating me on
the head. I lost a shoe running away from them.

I sneaked about till I got to the liquor store, got my
bottles of wine and picked up an Indian sweetheart
named Pauline. We went to an old broken-down house
and shacked up. Pauline, a jug of wine, and a few Salvation Army sandwiches, and I was happy as a seal at a
breathing hole, my aching head numbed. The next night
we got twelve jugs of wine and sat down to drink with ten
Indian friends from a reserve. It was the kind of party
that allows you to forget.

But Skid Row in Edmonton wasn't all just Indians
and Eskimos.

Sometimes I would drink with people from very re-
spectable families. There was a society lady who used to
party with us. She had troubles at home with her husband.
She stayed with me for a few days. And when she'd had
enough, she made me go to a phone booth with her. She
called her husband. She told him that the man who was
taking care of her was going to take her home. He said he
wanted to speak to me.

I took the phone and he said, "Okay, how much do I
owe you?"

I couldn't figure it out. Here was a man whose wife I
had been shacked up with for almost a week and he was
asking me how much money he owed me. Well, I was
broke as usual, so I said ninety bucks. I didn't think the
guy would really pay but when I got her home—they lived
away out on the northeast side of Edmonton—he was
sitting on the front porch crying and had the money in his
hand. She was happy to get home and he was crying mad
to get her back.

There were other high-society people. I remember meeting the president of a big business corporation. He drank because he hated firing people who couldn't do the jobs he hired them for. He worried about how their families would suffer. This kind gentleman ended up in a psychiatric ward. Once I even ran up against an understanding policeman. He was an RCMP corporal. He took me into a back alley and pulled out a bottle of whisky and we chatted for a long, long time. He was an alcoholic and didn't try to hide it. He knew the problems of the drunk because he *was* one.

I never met anybody on Skid Row who wanted to get off it. You always want to run out and find another drink. You get the money somehow, even if it means walking up to a stranger on the street and asking, "Sir, have you a dollar fifty for a bottle of wine?" I'd even bum a cigarette sometimes.

My carvings were my main income. When I was in the Charles Camsell Hospital, I would sell them to visitors. I made about twelve carvings the first time I was there. I got ninety bucks for the whole works. On Skid Row, I made carvings and I was stupid enough to sell them for the price of a bottle or a meal.

I met many women in Edmonton. Once I met two girls, one Indian and one white. The white girl was Dorothy. She was wild at lovemaking. The Indian girl told me that she was a nymphomaniac, and Dorothy said the Indian girl, Sylvia, was a dirty prostitute. They argued over me, but I satisfied them both the same night. I must have lost ten pounds doing it. I was told that a nymphomaniac is a girl who wants more and more sex, and can't ever get enough. Just like breeding rabbits, they jump from one man to another.

One time a Ukrainian girl asked me, "Tony, how do an Eskimo boy and girl have intercourse?"

At least she was nice and direct about it, so I showed

her some Eskimo tricks and she came back for more the next day. I told her that we sometimes have a problem when a man is smaller than the woman. Most Eskimo women are bigger than the men, so the girl takes the top position.

Another Ukrainian was the best woman I've ever had. She must have learned gymnastics. She could bend in any position. We stayed together for a week until her husband came back from the oil fields.

I always thought it was strange though, that I never met a woman who didn't drink or sell herself.

On many a morning I awoke in the drunk tank with a whole bunch from Skid Row. To wake up to filth and puke, men urinating on each other, is only a small part of the misery you face when you live in the street. Someone has a bowel movement on the floor of the cell and the smell, mixed with the breath of trench mouth, is sickening. You look toward a bunk a few feet away and a homosexual is trying to get into another guy's pants, masturbating on the floor. You hear the screams of men suffering from D.T.'s. You can't block it out, no matter how hard you try. Mean guys make it even tougher to take. I remember one time, there must have been twenty of us lying around, throwing up, and pissing and shitting on the floor. A guy came in and he was looking for a fight. He started kicking, and he hit one little drunk. Blood started coming from the little guy's mouth. He kicked a couple of other guys as he moved around the cell. I started to get up, slowly, and he tried to kick me, too. So I gave him three . . . four . . . five bad ones, rabbit chops, and he was down. I was learning to protect myself. And then the guard appeared and we all filed out to court.

Later you stumble outside into the damp air and head down to the Sally Ann or the mission and join the soup line. You listen to the street gossip, how old so-and-so died from alcohol poisoning the night before, but it has no meaning for you. You don't realize you're heading down the same path.

There's violence everywhere. One night just before sunset, I was walking down 96th Street with an Indian boy from the north country. I noticed something on the road ahead just after turning the corner. We both saw it at the same time.

"Look at that," I said. "Some guy sleeping?"

We went closer. The Indian boy froze, his face suddenly almost as pale as a white man's. He started puking. The guy wasn't asleep at all. His head was half gone. A big block of wood, five by five lumber, lay on the road. Someone had smashed his skull open. Blood was splattered over the pavement, and there was a pool of it where the boy lay. I was sick, too, from seeing a man's brains coming out. I went straight to the liquor store and covered my mind with a few drinks.

Often, in the street, I'd see guys coming along all beat up, blood running down their clothes. And when I'd look at them, I'd sometimes wonder how they could be out walking in that condition. And yet, when I'd get drunk myself, get robbed and beaten, I'd be just like them. And I wouldn't even think to look in a mirror.

I still saw Riverbank Mary, and one day on 96th Street I met my friend, Archie Starr, a Cree Indian. He was plastered drunk and all set to marry her. He couldn't see straight so I hitched him up to another Mary, a girl called Midnight Mary, a hooker. When he woke up alongside of her the next morning, he was madder than hell.

But I didn't care. I still had Riverbank Mary, and some wine, and I could laugh till the end of the world. After spending the night and most of the next day with Mary, I went to the Sally Ann for a meal. Then I sold my watch for $5.67. I bought five bottles of Berry Cup wine and sat and drank by myself down by the river.

I thought about the North, while I drank, and the way it was up there in summer, long before I was born . . .

This family lived by the sea shore in a skin tent called a tupek. A man, a woman, and a little boy. The man is thinking that the winter past was hard but good. He hunted nanook and lost some dogs. Nanook is tough, and the man and his family are hungry. But they still have six good dogs left, and some dried caribou meat, mipku. I have to go and fix my kayak frame, he thinks.

He lights the lamp with flint and makes a fire with seal oil. Then he works and watches the sea. There are big waves and seals which will make fine skins for his kayak, and meat for the family. Eider ducks swim on the ocean, and he can hear the call of the King Loon on the sea. The man's wife is awake now and before he goes to hunt ducks, he rubs his face on the side of her neck to make her happy.

His kayak is ready and he takes his harpoon and duck spear and loads them on top of the boat. He carries his bow and arrows. He harpoons a seal and shoots a duck and he knows his family will eat well. As he paddles home, he remembers how he met his woman and had to prove his manhood to get her. She is the daughter of a chief far away and the chief told him to get a fresh nanook skin and a real white mountain sheep skin. The man had to hunt the polar bear on the ice, then go inland to hunt the mountain sheep. He shot it with a bone-tipped arrow. The chief was happy and he gave the man his daughter.

Now the hunter is home, and his son takes the eider ducks while his strong wife drags up the seal. The man carries the kayak up to where the sea can't reach it. The woman skins the seal and stretches the skin on the ground. She says "Koyanangayain Iepung" . . . I thank you very much, my partner, my man. Then she plucks the eider duck and boils it. She gives the dogs seal blubber to eat . . .

The next day at the liquor store, I was hit over the head and robbed of a bottle of wine and eight dollars. My head was all bloody, and my leg hurt. I went to the student's clinic and they washed my head and cleaned the wounds on my leg. All summer long my left leg stank and the skin rotted off. They wouldn't let me into the Charles Camsell Hospital because I was drunk. Out on the street the flies used to get at my head because of the wound, and my hair started coming off. I washed the wound with rubbing alcohol and it cleared up in time.

The deeper I got into Skid Row and liquor, the more I would dream of the North.

I was alone with my grandfather on a piece of ice that had broken away from the shore. My father could not get to us because the storm was bad and the ice kept drifting farther and farther out. We built an igloo that was snug and warm, and grandfather got a seal.

But one morning I could not awaken him. Our fire went out and it was cold, very cold. I couldn't cook so I ate raw seal meat and fat. Then I crawled back beside my grandfather to sleep. For many days I was weak, cold and stiff, and my grandfather still would not awaken. Six days passed and still he slept. Each time I got hungry I would crawl to the raw seal meat and fat, frozen cold. I tried to wake up grandpa but his body was hard, like a dead seal. My caribou skins kept me alive and at last my dad came with my brothers . . .

The dream left me with a message. Only the wind cries for my people who suffer. No one knows about them.

13

Charged with Murder

I had to get out of Edmonton for a while. This judge—I'd been up in front of him about six times for being drunk— he told me if I ever showed up in his court again, he'd put me back in that nut house. I told him it had helped me before and I could use it again. But he shook his head and told me I had two hours to get out of town.

I went hitch-hiking with an Indian guy called Pete Hope. It was the first time I'd ever travelled that way. We walked pretty near six miles before getting a ride. Going along the road, we got thirsty and stopped in front of a farm. There was a little ditch coming out of it. The ditch ran alongside the road and I went down into it. I was going to take a drink but I smelled something and when I looked I saw animal stuff floating in it. Then Pete came jumping down into that ditch and he didn't wait for anything. Before I could warn him, he had ducked down and taken a real big drink. Then he stood up and he was sick all over. The ditch was full of cow shit and Pete got a real mouthful.

Just then, the good farm people saw us and came over. When they saw we were only a couple of poor, hungry natives, they made us welcome and brought us out a meal. A bunch of sandwiches, some vegetables, and some milk. Our stomachs were full after that, and we took to the road again.

This time we got a ride, with a businessman in a big blue car. Boy, he was in a hurry! He was travelling over a hundred miles an hour, and we nearly hit a few cars on the road. But Pete and I had some wine and that calmed us down.

We drove through Calgary and right on to Lethbridge.

I got mixed up with a whole bunch of Blackfoot Indians in Lethbridge, soon after arriving. They weren't too welcome in bars. So they did their drinking in a park. A big one. You could camp in one park and picnic in another. We put all our money together and one of the guys went away to the bootlegger's to fetch some booze. When he came back his arms were full of bottles. It was a different kind of liquor. Bay rum. We all just sat there and had a big party. We drank all afternoon and into the night. We were making lots of noise, too. And the police came, shining their torches in our eyes. I didn't know it was against city laws to drink in a park. We were taken down to the police station, about thirty of us, in the back of a couple of paddy wagons. But they didn't lock us up. They just took our names and told us to go.

For a whole week I slept in that park under the trees with those Indians. They were sleeping there, so I did too. I thought that's where everybody slept in Lethbridge. The Indian people brought food—big chunks of meat. We'd take it down to the lower valley of the park where there was a cooking place and make a fire and roast it.

Sometimes I'd wander off by myself and on one of those trips I met some cowboys. They said they were from the Calgary Stampede. I did a bit of work for them— helped them move stuff, cleaned up the stables where the horses were, picked up garbage around the place.

A few days later, the cowboys left and I hitched a ride to Fort Macleod. A good family of Blackfoot Indians took me in out of pity when they found me sleeping outside in the cold. It wasn't really cold for me but they thought it was. They took me onto their reserve, right into their farmhouse. They asked me questions about why the Eskimo has white man's rights and not the Indian. I told them it is because we never signed a Treaty with the white man. We never fought the wars that Indians and whites fought in the South, so we have our own rights, I said, but not the rights to oil, or land or minerals, because the white man can just come in and take them away. The only rights we have are liquor rights. The Indians, I said, have a better deal but they do have less freedom away from their reserves.

I had a good job there.

I was cutting hay and piling it, and moving cows around, and lots of horses. Sometimes, I'd haul hay into Fort Macleod from the reserve.

I found some soapstone near the reserve and did some carvings in my evening hours because the children wanted to know more about Eskimo ways. With wood I found in the bushes I made some bows and arrows. It was good with the children there. I didn't have time to drink too much because I was looking after them in a way.

But that good life didn't last long. After a while, there was no more hay to cut. No more work for me. So I headed back to Lethbridge and I was bumming again.

I got work with a company making trailers. My job was putting in door and window frames. I did that for a few weeks during the winter. It was kind of nice to have steady money coming in. I even opened a charge account at a store. Well, sort of a charge account. I went into the store just before pay day. I wanted a pack of cigarettes but I was a few cents short. The storekeeper had me sign my name in a little book and he gave me the cigarettes, saying I could pay him later. I never paid that good man back because when I got my cheque the next day, I couldn't cash it. None of us could. There was something wrong with the company's finances. A lot of Indians were on the payroll and they got real mad and started busting up the place. It came close to a riot. They were throwing stones and someone tried to set fire to the camp. I got out of there quick. I thought they were going to burn the place down. I didn't want to get hit on the head, either. My head was suffering enough.

I met two more Indian guys after that. They had a car and we drove around town drinking. Some time later, they stopped the car in front of a house and went in. When they came out, they were loaded down with big bags, with all sorts of stuff inside. I took a look in one of them and saw a fur coat. I pulled it out and put it on, but it looked silly, so I shoved it back in the bag. Just then I heard the roar of the car engine and the tires squealing. The two Indians just about knocked me into the ditch taking off down the road in that thing. The next moment I was grabbed from behind by two policemen. The Indians must have seen them coming. The dust hadn't even settled when I was locked in handcuffs and put in the back of a cruiser for the trip to the station.

I was charged with breaking and entering and theft. The police told me if I pleaded guilty, I'd only get three months and be able to serve my term in an alcoholic centre. I trusted them, but the judge was a Mormon potato farmer who hated drinkers. He gave me six months, and it wasn't in an alcoholic centre, either. It was in the Lethbridge Jail.

To tell you the truth, it wasn't that bad. I was bothered by the lack of freedom, all right. But it was a place to pass the rest of the winter. I worked in the kitchen and didn't have to eat all that cooked food at the long tables with the other men. I was able to eat right out of the fridge, all the frozen fish and meat I wanted. I had quite a bit to do to keep me out of trouble, with Alcoholics Anonymous meetings and doing some writing on my own time. There was no schooling but I would pick up a book once in a while and sort of go through it, studying it, and looking up words in a dictionary. That judge would sure be mad if he found out I didn't serve the six months he sentenced me to. They let me go on good behaviour after serving only half that time.

I had a little bit of money, given to me by the jail people, when I got out. I went to the bus depot and headed north, through Calgary, through Edmonton, and on to Peace River in Northern Alberta.

For a month, I worked for the highways department paving roads. When that ran out, I took a job that was completely new to me, working for the people who bring cow's milk to the North in cans. The dairy farm was six or seven miles out of Peace River. It was owned by a family from Switzerland. They were among the kindest people I met during those lonely years. They took a poor Eskimo in and treated him like he was one of them. The family was made up of a man and wife, their five children of six to fourteen years of age, and a grandmother. I milked sixty to seventy cows every morning and night-time. For the first while, I stayed outside in a little house by myself. But when a rainstorm came up, that little house wasn't much protection, so the family moved me inside with them. They gave me my own room upstairs in their place. They fed me well but I liked it best when we would all go into the bush and have a wiener roast. We did that a lot that summer.

Living with those Swiss people was for me happiness I hadn't known since leaving mission school on the Arctic coast. But I just couldn't stay away from the liquor. I never drank when I was on the dairy farm. But I would go into Peace River and get drunk sometimes. And those trips got more and more frequent. Finally, I just didn't come back. I missed that family bad but the booze took hold of me again and wouldn't let me go.

Back in Edmonton I looked up Riverbank Mary. She said, "Let's get some sniffing."

We went and bought Cutex and glue at a drug store down the street. The man handed us the Cutex out of a big cardboard box of bottles he had sitting right there on the front counter. Mary and I walked down a dark road and she got a bag and poured some of that stuff into it. We spent the night fooling around and making love and sniffing that stuff.

The next day we drank hair spray and rubbing alcohol, but eventually we got back to wine and we both ended up in a hospital with the D.T.'s. Actually, it was the alcoholic rehabilitation centre again. What a life, I thought. My craving for alcohol always made me hit the bottle and Skid Row. I am glad my dad never had to live on the street. I hope that most of my people won't have to either.

The alcoholic rehabilitation centre didn't help any. As soon as I got out, I was on the booze again.

From the liquor store, I headed for a bar looking for prostitutes. I hid my bottle in my jacket and walked into one. I could see a bunch of hookers sitting at the back, and I took a table near them. One of the hookers—her name was Donna—handed me a glass and I filled it up with rum from my bottle and had a drink. I was just starting to fill her glass, too, when the barman came over and told me I'd have to leave. I didn't want to fight so I got up and went outside.

To hell with it, I thought. I'll drink by myself. I wandered off down the road, drinking out of my bottle as I went. I was pretty drunk when I got to the scrap iron pile. I was going to go in there and sleep and dream of the North when I was a young hunter. But the red car was too fast for me. It came from behind and knocked me off the road. I saw it speeding into the darkness as I lost consciousness in the scrap iron pile. Hours—it could have been days—later, I crawled out from behind the scrap heap. I was hurting bad. At the hospital they told me to sit and wait until the doctor had time to see me. But I couldn't wait. I went out and got drunk, and I ended up in the city bucket.

I spent a day inside. Out on the street later, I met two policemen. One told me to beat it, but I told them I wasn't drunk. They were young cops. They put the handcuffs on me and threw me hard, head first, into the paddy wagon.

One of them got in with me. My arms were fastened behind my back with the iron cuffs. He put his foot on my back and forced my arms up to my neck. I howled with pain, but the policemen were laughing.

Something snapped in my right arm, also in my head. I blacked out.

I lost all track of time and feeling. I don't know how I got to the Charles Camsell Hospital. Maybe somebody brought me there. I came to, and my right arm was real big, filled with blood poisoning. I was reeling with the pain, and when the doctor arrived to look at me, I couldn't stand it any more. I tore my elbow open with my left hand. I was half out of my mind. Pus filled a basin, mixed with pink blood. It was rotten, green and yellow. The pus had reached my shoulder and my wrist, and the policeman with his foot on my back was still vivid in my memory. I could hear the snap—my arm.

I don't remember much of my stay in the hospital. I only remember leaving it, heading for the bus depot and being told by two Blackfoot Indian girls that someone in Edmonton was out to get me. I left for Lethbridge with the girls.

I was hoping to collect that week's wages owed to me by the trailer company. I planned to pick up the pay and go back home to the North, and try to start all over again.

But we started drinking on the bus and only got as far

as Calgary. I got a room in a hotel. It cost me fifty dollars, because that night three Indian guys broke, in, beat me up, and smashed the room. I had to pay the damage.

I was picked up again for being drunk. At the police station they told me take my jacket off. Instead of giving me time to take it off, they grabbed me and tried to rip it off. A bunch of policemen threw me to the floor. Three of them held me down and a fourth kicked with his heel. It ripped my throat open. They threw me in a cell and I tried to hang myself because I thought I was just as good as dead anyway. I tore off my T-shirt and made a rope out of it. I climbed up and tied one end to the top of the cell, the other end around my neck and just let go. I don't know what happened after that. I don't remember being cut down or anything. But the police must have—somebody must have cut me down. I came to my senses in the morning. I was lying on the bed in the same cell. The T-shirt was gone, all my clothes were gone. Then a policeman came and I was released to the street.

It was about eight-thirty in the morning. I met a girl named Rowena Crane Bear and we went to the bootlegger's and got two bottles of wine. We drank together all day. I remember Rowena and I stopped a fight. Two women and two men were beating up an old man. Later, we left for the Queen's Hotel bar where we sat until 3:30 p.m. I had two bottles of wine on me. Another girl, Christine, came in and said she knew where we could go. And we left . . . Rowena, Christine and I. Out on the street, Christine wanted to walk on my right-hand side, and I remember Rowena asking her why she wanted to. They argued about it. I was going to shack up with Rowena. Christine took us to a room. I was quite high. I remember there were eight or ten women, and one man—myself. I passed around the two bottles, and when I took my first drink, I lost sense of everything.

When I came to, I was in the city bucket, with no

clothes on. My head was really sore. Later, the police transferred me to a smaller cell. I asked them what they had picked me up for, and they told me it was on a drunk charge. But they were watching me all the time, and I asked them why. Two days later, I was charged with non-capital murder. Two detectives came in. They gave me a new suit, a white shirt and black shoes, and put me in a line-up with some white men and two little Indians. I looked like a crow among a bunch of white people. I didn't know what it was all about.

Later, two detectives questioned me.

One said, "Tony, you are an intelligent man, so tell us all you know about the 6th of November, between say, five and six o'clock ... where you were, and what you were doing?"

I told them of the two girls, and of not knowing anything from the time I took that drink of wine.

They asked me if I knew Charles Ratkovitch. I told them I did not know him. When I told the two detectives that I couldn't remember killing anyone, one of them kept saying, "It's a good crutch". He said it over and over again. It didn't make any sense to me. Then they told me, "You, Anthony Apakark Thrasher, are charged with non-capital murder." I didn't believe them.

That night, I dreamed of a future that would never come.

The land is covered in blue darkness, a dim glow comes from the Northern Lights and the stars. Late October, the big timber wolves are drifting from the inland to the Arctic barren lands to hunt the caribou. I can see them and I can hear them howl. The howl is lonely but lovely to listen to.

I am on a trapline with a great catch of white foxes, worth three thousand dollars. I trek back to the village and there is a big party to celebrate my good fortune.

When everybody has gone home, I walk into my igloo.

Gabrielle is waiting for me. The two of us find ourselves close to each other as we talk and laugh. There is silence suddenly, and our hands are warm and wrapped together. The North Wind blows outside. A blizzard. The dogs howl until sleep catches them. Gabrielle and I are side by side, in bed alone. We warm each other with our love until our hearts beats are out of control. Sweet, sweet love. In a flash, I am married to Gabrielle. Life is beautiful. All is love and happiness . . .

The crash of a cell door destroyed my dream forever.

A policeman was shouting at me to get up. I was being transferred to Spy Hill Jail where I would remain until the end of my trial. Spy Hill is a squat little place in a valley in the rolling hills west of Calgary.

I was put in a small holding room with a dozen other guys brought to Spy Hill that day. We were signed in one by one, taken to a washroom to change into jail clothing, then each was given a cell.

My cellblock was mostly for hard cases. All kinds of tough guys were in there. All on "remand" like myself.

At night I was locked in my cell, but at seven in the morning a guard would come and unlock my door and I'd have to rub shoulders with those guys all day in the ward until I was locked up again in the evening. Some of them were insane, really out of their minds. They had chips on their shoulders and were always trying to pick fights.

One of them was in for stabbing a man a hundred and twenty-five times. He wasn't too bad with me, but he was wicked with everybody else. Every chance he got he tried to grab a weapon to use on the next guy, whoever was closest.

As a way of protecting myself, I took up weight-lifting. Before long, I was pressing 300 pounds and I was as strong as a polar bear.

I soon found that guys charged with sex offences were coming around, trying to get me to guard them against attacks by other inmates. I saw one sex offender get it right in the holding room one day. They didn't even wait for him to be put in the cellblock. They just punched him out right there.

I don't remember what day I went to court first, but the judge said, "You are charged with the killing of Charles Ratkovitch." I still couldn't believe it.

They showed me a picture of the man I was supposed to have killed. I couldn't remember ever seeing him in my life. All I could recall was something like a dream, a dream in my mind, like a girl crying. But I don't expect anyone to believe in dreams.

That night, alone in my cell, I heard my name mentioned on the radio. The Calgary radio station was painting a big, dirty picture of me. To them, I was a murderer. They knew nothing about my life, only what the police said in court.

It made me wonder what was going to happen to me. The thought of being hanged went through my mind. If I were alone in the world, I remember thinking, it would be okay to be hanged. But what about my family, those who love and care for me. I couldn't stand the thought of the hurt I would be causing them, the embarrassment.

I was getting letters from my little sister, Agnes. She was named after my other sister who died. It was comforting to get Agnes' letters, sent down from the North. The only visits I ever got were from my legal aid lawyer, William Stilwell. My little niece, Bernadette, sent me her love in one of Agnes' letters. I had never met Bernadette but I kissed her words on the page and I longed for the day that I could see her and hug her and give her all my love.

But then I thought, "That day may never come."

Agnes told me how my stepmother had lost her sight,

from drinking something, and was in a hospital in Saskatchewan. I knew that drink, from the white whalers at Herschel Island, had taken my real mother, too.

Christmas came, and then New Year of 1970. To pass the time, I played poker for candies brought in by the Salvation Army. I wonder what the Salvation Army priest would have said if he found out what I was using his candies for!

Six months after arriving at Spy Hill, I was found guilty of a reduced charge of manslaughter. Jeepers— that's a long word, like Tuktoyaktuk. I was sentenced to be locked up for fifteen years. Two months later, an appeal court reduced it to seven.

Part Four

Inside

14

A Devil's Castle

With a deafening roar, the RCMP Otter lurched into the air and began a slow climb away from the airport in Edmonton. As the pilot fixed on a course for Saskatchewan and the Prince Albert Penitentiary, the huge CN building fell away from view and the roar of the engine faded to a steady drone. Every once in a while I would catch a look beneath the low clouds at summer-green wheatfields and I would think back on the happy, carefree days I spent with the Blackfoot Indian family on the reserve near Fort Macleod. The same melancholy thoughts had run through my mind earlier in the day in the police car as it moved along the black ribbon of asphalt cutting through the broad wheatfields between Calgary and Edmonton.

I was no better than a caged animal now, being flown across the country in mid-June of 1970 with eleven other prisoners, handcuffed in pairs. We had to raise our voices to be heard over the engine, and every so often the guards up front would shout at us to quiet down.

Three or four hours later, we bumped down at Prince Albert airport where we were put aboard a prison bus for the ten-mile ride to the penitentiary. Through the wire screens covering the windows, I could see groves of pine trees sweeping by on either side of the road. We crossed over the North Saskatchewan River, murky with silt, and continued through the town of Prince Albert, and a few minutes later I heard the driver gearing down. The big, sixty-year-old red brick institution which is the Prince Albert Penitentiary was in the clearing ahead.

The sun hid itself behind angry, black clouds and I could hear thunder overhead and flashes lit up the sky. As the dark blue bus rolled to a stop in front of the main iron gate, the rain was splashing the window. I was soaking wet by the time they marched us through the gate and across the yard on the other side of the high outer wall to the main prison building. In an upstairs reception room, we showered and changed into prison clothing. Then the guards led us down a long hospital-green corridor that came out on the edge of a deep concrete and steel cavern they called the dome. We walked down three flights of black metal stairs to the bottom and I could see, behind barred gates, in front and to the right and left of me the long, narrow cellblocks, four tiers high. Here and there, prisoners stood leaning over the black railings running the length of each tier. In a cage, up near the top of the dome, a guard perched with a rifle by his side. Through the long, barred windows cut into the outer walls of the cellblocks, I could see the sky flickering as the electrical storm continued and I could hear the black clouds rumbling—the sound mixed with the echo of men's voices in that locked tomb.

A guard nodded for me to follow. They opened one of the barred gates and I was escorted to a cell on the bottom tier of the cellblock to the right of the dome. As I entered the cell, I could hear the crashing of the barred gate being locked shut behind me. The little enclosure was to be my home for the next thirteen months. There wasn't much. A narrow bunk fixed to the plastered wall. At the rear of the cell, a toilet, a locker for my personal effects, and a stained washbasin. A little reading lamp and a tiny writing table against the wall opposite the bunk.

I had never been in a place like this before. Spy Hill was bad enough, but P.A. was like a devil's castle. In the grimy, stinking walls of the long, dimly-lit corridors, I could almost reach out and touch the shadowy forms of the evil spirits lurking there. I could almost hear their insane chatter with each echo of crashing steel.

That night, alone in my cell, I couldn't sleep at all. There was a Bible and I started thumbing through the pages in the semi-darkness, trying to read the words in the dim light glowing through the bars of the door. The book didn't make any sense. What could that do for me, I thought, in a place like this? I mean, with my freedom gone and years of suffering ahead.

Tossing and turning on the low, narrow cot, I tried to numb my mind with thoughts of my grandfather telling me stories of a long time ago. Countless times my mind would start to slip away from the grasp of the white man's prison only to be wrenched back by the sudden, chilling shriek of an inmate, crying out somewhere from the depths of some terrible nightmare.

As daylight began creeping through the dusty windows of the cellblock, activity outside my cell picked up. I could hear the night guards preparing to leave and join their families in the town and other guards coming to take their places in patrolling the wide landings outside the tiers of cells.

I washed my face and hands and then, a short time later, I heard the quiet-shattering clang of an alarm bell and the crash of steel. The guards were unlocking the cell doors, and I joined the other inmates in filing down to the kitchen to pick up our breakfast trays and return to the cells to eat.

That morning after returning my breakfast tray to the kitchen—they let me keep my cup and knife, fork and spoon in my cell—I noticed there was a tenseness in the cellblock that I didn't understand. A lot of inmates were walking slowly around with their shoulders hunched forward and their hands thrust deep in the pockets of their prison costumes, killing time before going to work. I was scared. I didn't know what was right to do and what was wrong. The prisoners had a code of behaviour and I didn't know it. All I knew was that you couldn't whistle to yourself. Whistling could get you a punch in the nose. I learned that in Lethbridge Jail.

An Indian I knew from the street came up to me and pointed to a guy leaning over the railing of the second tier from the top.

"Skinner," he whispered.

I should have known better but I didn't. I thought he was telling me the guy's name and, without thinking, I switched on a great big smile and shouted real loud . . .

"Hey, Skinner!"

The shuffling of feet on the polished concrete suddenly stopped. I could feel all those hunched shoulders turning slowly in my direction, all those angry faces fixing on me. I stood stock-still, like a young caribou cornered by hunters, trembling with fear and somehow knowing that to run would be useless. The voice of the Indian broke the tension. He was doing some fast talking to stop the inmates from closing in, explaining to them how I didn't know what a skinner was, how I didn't know "skinner" meant rapist. He was a good talker and they backed off. Then he took me aside and told me never again to act friendly toward the inmates on that tier. He called it the "protective custody" tier. If I did, he said, the inmates might kill me.

That was Lesson Number One in how to conduct myself to stay out of trouble. I didn't have to wait long for Lesson Number Two. It came that evening, after I'd spent the first day at school. The school was at one end of the gymnasium, reached through a long corridor from the dome. I picked out the subjects I wanted to learn—math, chemistry, English, some psychology. After supper I went out to the exercise yard. It was actually outside the wall of the main prison compound. A path from the gym let to it. When I went out, I saw there were hundreds of guys milling around there. After my experience in the morning I didn't much want to stay around them, so I looked towards the end of the yard where the wire fence was. There was nobody exercising over there so I started to walk over.

A guy grabbed my arm. "You go another step," he said, "and they're gonna shoot you."

I turned to him, puzzled. "Shoot *me*? Who . . . ? Why . . . ?"

He motioned to me to look up.

A quick look and I knew what he was talking about. On top of the towers. Guards with guns. If I tried anything, they'd shoot all right. I was between the devil and the deep blue sea and I didn't know how I was going to cope in that place for seven long years.

The only time I felt safe was at night when they locked me alone in my cell. I was a bundle of nerves and the prison doctors had to give me chloralhydrate so I could sleep.

There were madmen roaming that place. I never knew what was going on in their minds. I learned to watch for everything that moved and to be always on the alert for strange sounds behind me. At any moment, my life could end. The madmen didn't need a reason for killing.

For them, it could have been as simple as thinking, "There's an Eskimo. He's the only one in here. Might as well get rid of him."

Because of the ever-present danger, I continued to weight-lift, so I could defend myself if I had to. The gymnasium was a good one and I would go there often after supper and work out.

There were scores of Indians and half-breeds among

the prison population, and as another form of security, I joined the Native Brotherhood.

It was a good idea but it had its bad side.

Racial tension was running high between whites and Indians and niggers. As an Eskimo, I was in the middle. I didn't exactly fit into any of those groups. At the same time, I wasn't against any of them either. I chose the Brotherhood because I knew a lot of Indians up North and on the street. But joining meant I had to take the side of the Indians in any fight that took place.

And there were a lot of them.

15

So You Want to Kill an Eskimo

Even the summer breezes knew enough to stay out of Prince Albert Penitentiary.

More than once during August I almost collapsed from the heat. The cellblock was like the devil's furnace. My sweat soaked clear through my cheap, canvas prison outfit. Though I'd only see the sun when they'd let me out into the exercise yard each evening from six to nine-thirty, its energy crept into every room, locked in by the same high walls that kept everybody else inside that prison.

Whenever I got the chance, I'd sneak into the meat cooler in the kitchen. It was nice in there. But they kicked me out when they caught me. Other than the meat cooler, there was no place to escape. At night, the cellblock was impossible to sleep in. My bedding was wet. So was everybody else's. Even the cracked plaster of our cells was sweating. You could see drops of water streaking down from the ceiling.

The long, unbroken days of temperatures in the eighties were beginning to get to guys' minds in there.

More and more often you could hear screams in the night. Guys going crazy in their cells, stir crazy. They'd scream for a long time. Then you'd just hear muffled sobbing.

The guards, patrolling silently along the landing, seemed to sense the tension. Through the bars of my cell, I could see that they were more alert, their faces drawn, their eyes flicking from cell to cell.

Then it happened.

A nigger guy slashed an Indian with a knife.

The effect on the exercise yard that evening was explosive. All the white guys and niggers began grouping together on one side of yard, the Indians and half-breeds on the other. They were getting set for a big brawl and it wasn't long in coming.

Somebody shouted that two niggers were cornered in the gym. It was all anybody needed.

A big gang of Indians ran from the yard toward the gym, with a gang of white guys and niggers in hot pursuit. I followed behind, and when I neared the gym I could see a full-scale riot had broken out.

Furniture was being smashed and blood from bashed noses was all over the place. I couldn't hear myself think for the screaming and shouting and thumping going on, so I figured I'd better get in there and help somebody.

I ripped off a table leg and went in swinging. When I saw more than two guys ganging up on a friend, I just put my stick in between them and broke it up. Soon guards began popping up here and there and guys were being dragged back to their cells to cool off. Within half an hour, it was all over. We were locked in our cells, none the worse for wear except for a few guys who got black eyes and busted noses.

That riot taught me something—the need to have a knife handy. I saw knives among some of the men in the gym. A lot of inmates seemed to have them hidden in their cells. I figured I'd better get myself one.

On a trip to the kitchen I grabbed a carving knife. To tell you the truth, I grabbed two. I had no trouble getting by the guards with the knives tucked under my shirt.

They seemed to trust me a lot. I guess it was because I never gave them trouble as other inmates did.

That week, those knives saved my life.

It was a quiet afternoon and I was dozing in my cell after finishing some school work. It must have been my hunter's instinct. There wasn't exactly a sound, but I was suddenly aware of some action behind me.

Without giving it a second thought, I sprang from my cot and faced the door.

Standing there were five big Indians.

"White-lover," the tall one said quietly, so the guards couldn't hear. I could see the steel glinting in his clenched fist. The others had them, too. Cell-sharpened table knives.

They said they were going to kill me because I took the side of the whites in the riot. I had never heard of such silly business. All I'd done was keep some guys from being smashed up. But I wasn't going to stand there and argue with them.

I could smell something on their breath, and their eyes were glassy. I guessed it was extract from the kitchen. They didn't seem too steady on their feet and I figured, in their drunken state, I could probably move quicker than they could.

Bounding to the rear of my cell, I grabbed up my carving knives, one in each hand. Those Indians didn't have a chance to get to me.

"Okay, you heroes," I said, crouched, ready to spring. "So you want to murder an Eskimo. Let's see you try . . . "

I've skinned a lot of animals in my life. Those five animals, I figured, I could skin them easy enough, too.

"Well . . . what do you say?"

They didn't say anything. They were too busy staring at my two big meat cutters to answer. It was enough for them. They turned and fled back to their cellblock. I never had any trouble with them after that.

A lot of strange things went on in that prison.

There was one cellblock, for instance, where the bottom tier was a mixture of Indians, whites and niggers. In the top tier, all the guys were Indians. The one below that had Indians and half-breeds. And the one below that was the most interesting.

It was full of queers.

A guy in there borrowed my chest-expansion springs and I took a walk through to get them back. I laughed at what I saw, but deep down inside I felt sick. Those homosexuals were mixing it up in there.

There was a lot of it in that prison, in most prisons, I guess. When society locks men up without women for long stretches, they go kind of crazy.

You could see unnatural acts anytime, almost anywhere, inside the walls of Prince Albert Penitentiary.

The auditorium, in the same building as the gym, was where they held evening movies. I went a couple of times. But I stopped going after I saw what went on in there.

It was a laugh. Not the films but what would happen in the seats around me after the lights went off. Guys wouldn't even look at the screen. They'd be squinting around the darkened theatre looking for their lovers or new "sweethearts" to screw. Right beside me once I looked down and a guy was there on his hands and knees, giving the inmate next to me a blow job.

Homosexuality. I couldn't even escape it when I attended Alcoholics Anonymous meetings. One night this big half-breed guy came to a meeting and I saw him go into the washroom at the back of the room. Soon a lot of guys were filing in there. They were taking turns with the half-breed. A guard eventually caught on to their little game and they were kicked out of the AA program.

There were even male prostitute rings in Prince Albert.

Good-looking guys were selling themselves for as

much as fifty dollars a crack. They had pimps to protect them, just like girl prostitutes on the street.

Some of the younger boys were unwilling victims of the bigger, tougher inmates. It was commonplace to see them being dragged into a cell by three or four big toughs and gang-raped. You'd hear a muffled scream and you'd know it was going on.

For some guys, the thought of living with that, day after day, night after night, knowing there was nothing they could do to stop it, was too much for them. They snapped.

A friend of mine, a young Indian, said to me one day, "Hey Tony, I'd like to give you some stuff."

"Sure, okay," I said.

He gave me his art outfit—all his pencils and brushes and paints and paper. I put them in my cell. And he shook hands with me.

"See you again some day, buddy," he said, and he went back inside his cell. I thought maybe he was going to do something about getting out of that place, like going over the wall.

I went to sleep that night. I didn't hear a thing.

Nothing.

And in the morning, when the cell door opened, I saw there was blood coming out of the next cell. I peeked around the corner and looked in. He was lying at the back, on the floor. Lifeless.

The letters he had written to the prison bosses, asking for a transfer or early parole, had done him no good. The bosses in Ottawa had turned him down. So he slashed himself. No sound or anything. Just ended it quietly. At least he didn't have to put up with those madmen anymore.

Three guys committed suicide at Prince Albert within a year and a half. Twenty-four other guys didn't quite succeed, out of a population of 370 prisoners.

The money to pay prostitutes came through dope dealing. Dope dealing and prostitutes. They were the two biggest rackets inside that pen.

There was an inmate there who had more than ten thousand dollars on him—in cash. I saw it with my own eyes. Friends on the outside were smuggling dope in to him. Sometimes a guard would help.

Much of the violence in the penitentiary stemmed from drug transactions. Those guys really played for keeps. I'll give you an example.

Towards the fall, I had to go into Holy Family Hospital in town for an operation on my neck where that policeman had dug in his heel. After surgery I was wheeled into a side room to give the wound a chance to heal. While I was lying there, I heard a commotion, and I looked up to see two nurses struggling to pull a bed into the room. There was a guy in it. He was unconscious and there were tubes connected to him. I guess to keep him alive. The nurses went out, leaving him in the room with me. I could see that he was beaten up bad.

A few minutes later, the door opened. An RCMP officer poked his head in. The policeman looked at the unconscious guy, then at me. Then a sudden, horrified look came over his face and he ducked out of sight. I could hear him running down the corridor. Thirty seconds later, he was back with the nurses.

"Get him out of here," he ordered, pointing to the unconscious man.

The policeman's action didn't make any sense to me. But the next day when I was returned to the prison, an inmate's questioning made it all clear.

He caught up to me as I made my way to school. He was out of breath and could hardly get the question out.

"Did you see that man in the hospital?"

"Yah! What happened to him? He was all beat up!"

He told me how the guy had stolen money from a

dope dealer, then ratted to the guards about the dealer after being caught with the loot.

Friends of the dealer got him up against a wall in the darkened auditorium during a movie. They were trying to beat him to death but a guard stopped the execution at the last moment.

As the inmate told me this, he kept looking around nervously, as if frightened someone might overhear him and tie him into the plot.

Suddenly he looked at me directly.

"You finished him off, didn't you?" he asked, as if there was only one answer.

"No."

He heard but he didn't believe.

"What?"

I repeated my answer. "No, I didn't finish him off."

The inmate's eyes narrowed and he looked at me for a long time. Then he shook his head and took off down the long corridor. I saw him disappearing into a crowd of inmates near the cellblocks. He was still shaking his head. In a prison like P.A., killing is one of the things you're expected to do, I guess, when someone breaks the code.

I had to unleash some of my feelings. And I did, on the football field.

All that fall, the inmates played football in the exercise yard in the evenings. They had teams. A lot of the prisoners would go down and watch the action, even the guards. I was usually busy in my cell with my school work. But with all the trouble I was getting into around that place, I couldn't think straight, so one night I went down to see a game.

It was really exciting, with a lot of shouting and screaming and people jumping up and down on the sidelines, cheering for their favourite team. Some silly guys were even taking bets. I had never played football but I had watched the big professional teams on television.

It looked easy enough, so the next night I jumped into a game.

Boy, when you're out there playing, it sure is different from when you're watching. I was on the Indian team and they were playing the real professional stuff, without padding. The nurses were on the sidelines, waiting with stretchers, and we were tackling, jumping, and knocking each other all over the field. The others were playing rough, so I played rough, too.

Somebody kicked the ball in the air and I saw a guy catch it. He was taking off with it, down the field. It was my big chance to show all those white guys that an Eskimo can play football, too. I took off after him like a wolf after a reindeer.

When I got close behind, I leaped just like I'd seen the professionals do. I was going to grab him by the legs and pull him down. But I was flying too high for that. Must have flown quite a few feet in the air, because when I hit him it was straight in the back—with my head. When I came to on the ground, they were carrying him off the field on a stretcher. He had a broken shoulder blade and three cracked ribs. I thought they'd charge me for sure, for doing that to him. But they didn't. They never charged the football players because it was only sports.

The Indians wanted me to play a lot of games after that. I did. It helped to calm me down. But it wasn't the answer to my problems. The madmen, the drug pushers, the homosexuals were still coming around.

Sometimes I couldn't even eat my supper in peace.

I'd bring my tray to my cell from the kitchen and guys would gather outside my door. They'd be asking for my dessert and vegetables.

They wanted it for making homebrew.

It was easy to make in there. Sometimes I'd make it myself. Time passed quickly when I had some homebrew in me.

How to make it? Get a plastic bag and put potatoes or any kind of fruit in it. Add water, sugar, and some yeast from the kitchen, and let it ferment in the back of your cell. Makes a good after-supper drink when there's nothing else to ease your pain.

But most nights I was cold sober when the lights went out at ten and I'd need my medication—the red-coloured chloralhydrate that the prison psychiatrist okayed for me. He was a nice old fellow, that doctor. He was all alone in the big prison. He did his best but, with all those guys needing him, all he could do was hand out something to tide us over, a little bit of medication. I was thankful to him for that. It cut my mind off from that place for a few minutes a night anyway.

But there were problems with the chloralhydrate, too.

The drug addicts wanted it. Many a night I went without sleep because I traded it to them for tobacco. Not for the tobacco but just to get rid of them.

16

Riot

When I was in Spy Hill, I spent most of my days and nights in my cell, putting my thoughts down on paper. My lawyer, William Stilwell, told me: "Recall everything you can, Tony." It was something to do to pass the time, and it was also a way of educating myself. And I thought that maybe some day my writing would be read by Eskimo children and they would know what to watch out for, so they wouldn't end up like me, in a white man's cage. When I began to write, I didn't even know about putting periods after sentences and beginning new ones with capital letters. I learned all that and much more by myself in Spy Hill.

But in Prince Albert Penitentiary, though I would have liked to write, I couldn't. I couldn't in there, because whatever words I might put down could put my life in danger. About all I could do was write short letters to Agnes. I could not really tell her much about what was going on in there, how my mental condition was getting worse, but I told her about the little things, like how when the prison's quiet and you're alone in your cell, you can hear birds, birds roosting high up in the dome. Mother and father birds, having little ones, living natural lives, while down in the bowels of the prison men are cut off from natural love, from their families, and their minds become twisted like the old hollow wrecks of cars I used to see in the junk yards of Edmonton.

By November, snow covered the exercise yard and the cellblock was cold and damp. It didn't bother me much. Neither did it bother Little Adam, another Eskimo, a small guy from the Eastern Arctic. He was admitted some time in the fall. The cold was nothing compared to what we'd been in before. But the poor white guys, stamping their feet out in the exercise yard, they were freezing.

"It's good for you," I'd shout to the tiny huddles of snotty noses, an ear-to-ear smile on my face. Little Adam would just grin shyly when I'd say that. He was scared in that place. I was too, but I tried not to show it.

A crazy thing happened later in the month. Eleven guys took off through a hole in the fence of the exercise yard. The guards in the towers didn't even see them go. So three more slipped through the fence, went to town and got booze and came back through the same hole. The guards caught the eleven but they didn't even know the three others had been out, too.

Because of the escape, some of our privileges were taken away. It touched off the tension again. Even the tough guys were edgy. You couldn't look sideways at them without getting a threatening look.

Little fights started breaking out again, mostly between whites and Indians, and men were plotting against the guards. The racial groups were separating again, getting ready for something big.

The next morning I was on my way out to the exercise yard when a guard stopped me and said I couldn't go out. I looked past him and I could see guys in the middle of the yard. They were just sitting there with guards around them. I didn't know what that was all about.

That night they locked us in our cells early. I put in my earpiece and heard the radio operator going on about the inmates in the exercise yard being on "hunger strike", whatever that was. He said it was because the warden wouldn't make improvements in the canteen. I knew it was because of the racial problems.

That night the tension grew to the boiling point. Prisoners started swearing at guards from their locked cells. The shouting increased. Soon all the guys were at the front of their cells, striking the bars with cups and spoons and shoes, and rocks smuggled up from the yard. . . anything they could find to make a noise with.

I could hear guys in other cellblocks doing the same thing. In that enclosed space, the noise was deafening. All night long, the clatter kept up. And, in the morning, the guards wouldn't let us out of the cells. We were kept locked up all day, as a sort of penance.

The next night, the banging of the bars began again, and we were locked up for a second day. We couldn't go to the kitchen for our food trays and the guards wouldn't bring them to us. I was getting real hungry, but all I could do was sit there in my cell and hope for peace soon.

By the third day, the inmates had had enough. The constant crashing of steel died down and I was able to relax. I tried not to think about what might happen next. I knew the tension was still there. I knew the prisoners were quiet only because their stomachs were empty.

That afternoon, the guards unlocked the cells and we raced down to the kitchen and filled up on supper.

After supper, the delayed blast came.

Somebody came running into the gym yelling that inmates were busting up the carpentry shop, away off in the field outside the dome.

I raced out into the corridor. I could see a gang of yelling, shouting inmates, tearing down the corridor towards me from the cellblocks, jostling and shoving each other as they came running along. I was pinned against the wall as the crowd surged by me into the gym where the school was.

Little Adam was at my side. He was so scared, he couldn't move. I heard an inmate shout, "Let's close the school." And when I peeked inside the gym, I could tell they were in the school, picking up books and ripping them apart and throwing them around.

Suddenly the crowd started to move back and I could smell smoke, and see the shadows of flames flickering in the school. The inmates went wild. Shouting, screaming, they spilled out into the main floor area of the gym, smashing windows, throwing chairs, swinging clubs and lengths of pipe. Some guys were setting more fires. I looked around and saw Adam, as pale as a white man, shaking with fear. I knew this was no place for either of us, so silently I pushed Adam away from the gym. We walked fast, almost at a run, back along the long corridor, starting to fill with smoke. Guards were gathering at the end of the corridor and they let us through to our cells. I entered mine and sat there shivering. I figured that was the safest place. I was scared. Real scared. Sitting alone on my cot, I could hear gunshots. The guards were shooting at the rioting inmates. You could hear bullets bouncing off the walls of the gym and the cries of panicking inmates. Even in my cell, the smoke was heavy, choking me. Then the guards turned on the hoses, and water began filling the cellblock. My tier was covered with seven inches of water.

Sometime after that, the shooting stopped and the shouting died down and the guards hustled the inmates back to their cells and locked them in. The riot was over. I had somehow avoided being killed or badly injured and I thanked Saganna for saving me. Only one inmate was beaten up badly in that riot. He was a nigger who had raped a white girl. They caught him by the hospital, and he was almost dead when they finished with him. Six guys were put in the hole, in solitary confinement, for setting the fires.

Later that night, the guards came back. One at a time we were taken out of our cells and told to strip naked and lean over the railing of the landing. They threw everything out of our cells, then they searched us thoroughly.

I was told to bend over so they could check my asshole to find out if there was anything there. I don't know what they expected to find. They even checked the nigger boys' bushy haircuts.

Later that week, they passed us through a big machine, shaped like a "U", some sort of electrical gadget that searched your body to see if you've got any metal on you. I went through it and it started beeping. All the guards looked at me with tense faces. There was no weapon though—just a little medal, some kind of Catholic medal. I don't even know where I got it from.

The tension continued, with the tough guys in the prison baiting the guards almost every day. I glued my eyes to the school books.

I was studying what I wanted to study—not what *they* wanted me to. When I came in there, they showed me some books. I flipped through the pages. It was what I learned in mission school that last year in 1950 when I was in Grade VI. I knew about that junk. So I told them to jam it someplace. I told them I was going to learn what *I* wanted to learn. I was doing my own time. Those guys weren't doing it for me. So I took up Grade X right off the bat. I didn't take the books they put in my hand. I took the books *I* wanted to read.

Algebra and psychology were my favourites. I studied them, and picked them up pretty fast.

Psychology I liked even better than algebra. I guess because I could see examples around the penitentiary of what I was reading—guys showing the different kinds of behaviour that the university people presented to me in those books.

All that winter and spring, I studied hard and in the

evenings I would play hockey and go to AA meetings. I even joined the Toastmasters Club. My speeches never won me first prize or anything, but I got a lot of little scraps of paper, saying "Second-best Speaker". That's better than third-best, I guess.

In my speeches to native groups, I'd just expose the simple things about the Eskimo people and their fight against the white civilization in the South, how the Eskimo children are not being taught about the old ways, how they are losing their roots. I'd suggest how the education system could be changed, so that our Eskimo children would not forget about their ancestors and the way they lived to survive in the harsh North.

I tried keeping to myself as much as I could to avoid trouble with the other inmates. But it was tough. Even minding my own business was getting me into trouble.

Like the time I didn't kill that prisoner in hospital. I paid for it. The inmates started shouting my name to keep me awake.

"Thrasher, you asleep. . . ? Don't sleep, Thrasher. . . You fucking Eskimo. . . You short-assed rat-fink lover. . ."

They kept it up late into the night. I pulled the pillow over my head but it hardly muffled the ghostly shouts ricocheting around the darkened cellblock walls.

With my cell door locked, at least my body was safe from those faceless enemies, even if my mind wasn't.

On another night, lying in my cell with my earpiece listening to the country and western music, a request came over for me. The announcer was an inmate himself. He'd take requests for music, almost all of them from queers.

"And here's a tune," the announcer would say, "dedicated to Rhonda from Jimmie."

Well, everybody knew that Rhonda was a big hooker down in that tier, second from the bottom.

This request that came over for me was from some

inmates who wanted to get back at me for something. It was for a love song and they dedicated it "To Tony from Suzie." In the morning, the inmates were making jokes about it as we lined up for our breakfast trays. They talked real loud so everybody could hear. All the inmates were laughing. I could only grin like a little boy and look for a place to hide. But there wasn't one. There was nowhere to hide from the madmen in Prince Albert Pen.

I had to get out of there. I started writing to the Federal Government, to the Solicitor-General's Department, writing letters to officials telling them Prince Albert was no place for an Eskimo. Did they think I should hook up to the stinking asshole of a homosexual man? Get me out, I pleaded. Get me out of Canada's Queer City, with its gearboxes and drag queens with names like Suzie and Rhonda.

I needed to be free, to walk around, to see nature again, to trap and hunt in the old way. I didn't think I would last seven years in that place, behind that red brick wall that hid all beauty, mixing with the madmen who had it in for natives like me.

At the barbershop in the reception area, I had them cut my hair real short on top, in what you call a brush cut, and I grew an Oriental moustache, a Manchu moustache. I did it to protect myself, so I wouldn't be bothered by the other inmates as much. I know the Oriental background and history is a part of mine, from way back. But I must admit I felt ashamed when, after taking on my new look, a newly-arrived inmate came up to me and asked what I was.

"Chinese? Japanese ... ?" he asked.

"Yes, yes," I said quietly, without looking up.

I am a proud Eskimo and I didn't even have the courage to admit it. That night I cried softly in my cell and prayed that my people would forgive me ...

17

The Cork Pops

The wheels of the big Boeing jetliner, touching down at Abbotsford Airport near Matsqui in the Fraser Valley made a short, clipped sound, like a dog's yelp, and I woke up abruptly. The Air Canada pilot braked, turned, and started taxiing across the field toward a small group of hangars in the distance. I stretched and rubbed the sleep from my eyes. At thirty thousand feet over the Rockies, I had dreamt I was adrift on an ice floe with Gabrielle and a team of dogs. I wasn't afraid because she was with me to keep me warm and safe. Wide awake now, I had only to look around the long, tubular cabin to know it was impossible for me to be with Gabrielle, with any woman.

The jetliner. It was like a prison without bars. Like one of those ships the niggers in P.A. told me used to carry slaves from Black Africa, only this one sailed the skies and not the seas. All the seats closest to the portholes were filled with prisoners like myself. Forty-eight of us, we were headed for institutions in British Columbia on transfers from penitentiaries across Canada. Two seats to my right, a brown-uniformed guard, one of twenty on the plane, shifted restlessly in his aisle seat as the jet slowed to a stop in front of the low buildings. As the whine of the engines faded away, he and the other officers started getting up, stretching, searching their pockets for the handcuffs which they had taken off us when the plane lifted away from Prince Albert. In the sky, there's no need for handcuffs. Nobody's going to escape up there.

The forward door was opening and again I felt the unpleasant sensation of the metal ring being fastened tightly around my wrist. Leaving the plane, walking down the steps, I was fully aware of my lack of freedom. Strangers in the distance were watching curiously, watching the drab parade of lost souls, of which I was a part, spilling onto the tarmac in the warm afternoon sunshine.

My arm jerked helplessly on the short chain leash. I could hear the chain jingle lightly, as the inmate I was twinned to broke into a quick walk in response to the nudge of a guard.

At least I was no longer stuck in Prince Albert Pen. It was July of 1971 and I was on my way to serve out my sentence at a minimum security camp on Vancouver Island. Matsqui Prison was just a stopover.

The next morning early, they hustled me and a bunch of other inmates into the back of a Royal City bus and we started out for the ferry that was to take us across the Strait of Georgia to Swartz Bay near Victoria.

Once aboard, they let us out to roam. No handcuffs or anything. I felt free for the first time in a year and a half. I had been on boats before but never anything this big. It was a huge passenger ferry and there were lots of fancy people strolling along its wide decks. Lots of beautiful girls dressed in short summer skirts with cameras slung over their shoulders. They took pictures of the tiny, green-forested islands passing by on both sides of the ferry. From the railing, I could see seagulls gliding—some just inches above the rich, blue, white-capped water, others soaring gracefully high in the sky—their pure white forms glinting in the fresh morning sun like the pictures of angels in mission school, describing endless interlocking circles in dreamy pace with the boat, seesawing through the salt waves to the big island off the mainland of B.C.

From the ferry dock at Swartz Bay, it was just a short drive to the minimum security camp, William Head, which was to be my home.

Climbing down from the bus, I couldn't believe my eyes. *This* was a prison! There weren't even any walls. Just a skinny little wire fence and a driveway leading up to a group of barrack-type buildings nestled among tall oak trees, with huge pink and purple bushes growing up here and there.

I could see groups of inmates playing ball beneath the trees and the only guard in sight was asleep on a table. I thought he must be sick or something. It was the first guard I had ever seen like that.

Well, we were checked in and everything seemed all right, but when they took us to our quarters I sensed something right away. Some of the inmates were high on LSD and stuff like that and I could smell marijuana. I could sense danger. When they showed me my room, I could see it wasn't a cell where I could sleep in safety from the madmen. It was an open cubicle, no door at all, one of many cubicles in a long dormitory building.

After putting my little bit of luggage in my locker, I followed the others out to another building, a low one, which was the dining hall. It was like a café. Inmates worked in the kitchen and the food was pretty good. Not like the rot gut they splashed on your tray at Prince Albert. It was nice not to have to eat in my cell any more.

In the afternoon, I went with some of the newcomers to look around our new home. One of them, a tall skinny guy who said he was a university student in on a drug trafficking charge, told us the camp was a hundred acres big. I could see it was like a park, a small park jutting out into what I later learned was the Strait of Juan de Fuca.

"Used to be an old quarantine station," the university

student said.

He pointed to a high dock. I could see a number of inmates, sitting, legs dangling over the side, cans of bait beside them, lines dropping down into the salt water.

"The big ships from China," he said, "they used to come in here at the turn of the century full of immigrants coming to work in Canada. Maybe your grandfather was among them."

"Uhhh," I said, trying not to show my surprise. My short-cropped hair and droopy moustache really *did* make me look like a Chinaman. I figured I might as well tell the truth.

"Eskimo, I'm an Eskimo," I told him.

"Eskimo!" he said. Now *he* was surprised. "What in hell's name is an Eskimo doing way down here on the Pacific Coast?" he chuckled. "You're supposed to be up around the North Pole, aren't you?"

"I'm down here touring prisons as a personal favour to the Prime Minister of Canada—that fella Trudeau," I said, giving him a gummy grin. I'd left my teeth at Prince Albert Pen.

We all got a good laugh out of that one.

The next morning I reported to the front office and the job I got was what I wanted most—carving. Those first few weeks I spent every day in the art shop out behind the dormitory with my soapstone and equipment, making little scenes from the North. I sold some, too, to visitors. There were lots of visitors coming through the gate, wives and girlfriends of inmates, and social workers and people from the city of Victoria who came to help the inmates with their rehabilitation programs. I made about three hundred dollars selling carvings in those first few weeks.

I mostly hung around with the Indians. Late afternoon, we'd head down to a little float at the end of the dock and sit and fish for cod and salmon. I'd put them in the fridge inside the art shop and eat them when they were frozen solid. Even snagged an octopus once. It had arms five feet long. I tried to pull it in, but lost it.

Saw a crazy thing one day. This inmate who had come out of the B.C. Penitentiary, a big maximum-security place like P.A. near Vancouver, he snagged a dog fish, kind of a little shark. The inmate was mad at everything. He yanked that dog fish out of the water and threw it onto the dock. And he got out his pocket knife and he started slashing that fish to bits right there on the dock. He just kept slashing and slashing until it was just chunks of meat and blood lying there. And then he threw the chunks of fish into the water and stomped off towards the dormitory. Even in a minimum-security penitentiary, you're not really free, and it gets to you after a while.

Towards fall, it started getting dark early. We weren't supposed to be down at the dock after dark but I'd go down on the float anyway and dangle my little hook into the water. Sometimes I'd be down there all alone as late as nine-thirty. I stopped that nonsense when a guard came down one night.

He stood on top of the dock and shouted to me. "What you doing down there?"

"Fishing!"

"You're not supposed to be out here at night. Get up there before they see you." Himself, he didn't mind. But it was one of the rules, and it had to be obeyed.

I was getting to know the place well, and I could see what was going on, the little games the inmates were playing. Some of them were right out of the tough crowd at Prince Albert Pen, homosexuals, drug sellers. Their girlfriends weren't what you'd call sweet young things. They were bringing drugs in through the gate. The guards knew about the drugs, but they never did anything about it, because it was one way to control the whole bunch without weapons. The girls were in another business, too. Guys would pay them for sex, right there on prison property, they'd have it. You could see couples making love all over the place.

That LSD stuff. I bought some. Tried it. Downed it with a glass of water. There was something wrong with it. My cubicle turned into an Eskimo ice house. They were throwing dead people into it. The stiff corpses were piling around my bed. I could see their empty eyes staring at me. They were starting to come to life, their green arms with the flesh hanging off, coming towards me on the bed. I could feel their cold, clammy touch, my genitals being fondled. Their horrible faces contorted like putty into expressions of wild, wicked lust, as they made loud sucking noises with their thick, wet tongues. I could feel their long arms, like those of the octopus, snaking around my legs. I screamed in terror, and when I opened my eyes, the horrible forms were gone and my cubicle was normal again. I lay sobbing on my bed, curled up, with my legs tucked close to my body, and it wasn't until the first morning light crept in through the window that the drug drained out of me and I was able to sleep.

Sometime after that, I tried some marijuana. But eventually I quit experimenting with drugs because the guys who tried to turn me on—a lot of them were homo-sexuals—they'd wait until I started to get my lid off a bit, and then they'd try to turn me on to them, too. I stuck to booze. It was easy to get in there, as easy as getting drugs.

What kept me going more than anything in William Head were the visits I got from Heather and Bonnie. They were nurses from Victoria, volunteers who used to come into the prison to take part in our native rehabilitation program. We'd have lunches in the clearing in the trees where the picnic tables were. Heather especially meant a lot to me. A young Scottish girl, she seemed to care for me as no other woman did, except maybe my sister, Agnes, who was writing letters to me all the time. Heather encouraged me to write, and I became editor of the native newspaper in the camp. She seemed to know what the problems of natives were. She'd tell me how to behave, how to stay out of trouble.

Then one day something happened to destroy that relationship. It involved the drug traffickers.

They told her that if she didn't bring drugs in for them, they would do something to me. She told me this during one of our talks over coffee in the recreation hall. After that I found a letter on the writing table in one of the guy's rooms. It was a letter they planned to mail to Heather. It said that if she didn't deliver the goods, they'd kill me.

I told Heather we'd better not see each other for a while. She agreed and I left her alone. But as each day passed without her, I grew more edgy. My mind was bursting and I had to settle the score with those drug guys.

One night after I'd had a few drinks I walked into the dormitory. The two ring leaders were there and I let them have it. I punched the one guy hard in the face and his teeth flew across the room. He crumpled on the floor and I turned to the other guy, a dangerous little fellow who always carried a knife. I walloped him in the gut and when he went down I started kicking him, kicking with all my might. By this time, the first rascal had come to. I could see him out of the corner of my eye, scrambling on all fours to get out of there in one piece. I let him go. But the second guy, I just kept kicking him. Blood was coming out of his mouth and his ears. But I didn't care. He had it coming to him. And I had it to give him. I can let things build for a long time, but when the cork pops, my insides explode. All my frustration and pent-up anger. It just floods out. I can't stop it.

I kicked and kicked and kicked until the guards came running and somehow they pulled me out of that room and hauled me away . . .

18

I Laughed for Fifteen Days

I had finally graduated to the B.C. Pen—the Big House. I had heard so much about it from the inmates at Prince Albert, how it was nearly a hundred years old and all kinds of prison reform groups had recommended the place should be blown up and replaced by something a little more humane.

The B.C.P. is built high on a hill overlooking the sawmill town of New Westminster on the Fraser River. It's a big grey fortress and behind its high stone and mortar walls sit about five hundred inmates, counting the days till their sentences are up and they can walk through that huge iron front gate to freedom.

I arrived on November 17th, 1971, in the back of a paddy wagon from William Head. It was foggy outside and in the distance I could hear the mournful wails of tugboats shepherding their log booms under the huge arched girders of the Patullo Bridge. I was sober by then and my rage had subsided. I remember thinking, boy oh boy, Tony, drink and your damn bloody temper have landed you in the stew again.

They marched me into the main dome and once again I heard the crash of steel, glimpsed the silhouettes of seething men caged in long rows of barred cells stacked one on top of the other. I was taken down a long damp corridor away from the main cellblocks and up three flights of metal stairs to a room completely isolated from the rest of the prison.

The special custody unit. It was unlike any other cell-block tier I had ever been on. Tough, burly armed guards patrolled along metal catwalks suspended about two feet above the polished concrete floor. A protective covering of steel mesh separated the guards from the two rows of cells, built back to back. Behind the guards, no big windows to let in daylight. Only tiny slits cut into the thick plaster walls like you see in pictures of castles.

For a moment I stood there trying to take it all in, this new horrifying experience. Then I felt a hand on my shoulder and they were pushing me along the row of cells, past disembodied voices shouting crazed curses from behind steel doors. Midway down the row, I felt the hand on my shoulder again, yanking me to a stop in front of an open cell. They pushed me into it, barking at me to strip. They took my clothes and threw me some coveralls. The door slammed shut with a crash and I was all alone in that narrow hole. It was even tinier than a normal cell. Not much more than six to eight feet. The smell made me want to vomit—a combination of urine and disinfectant. No natural light and the light provided was dim. I looked around. Nothing. Just a heavy wooden built-up plank for a bed or to sit on. A pail to shit and piss in.

I was in there for a month. They didn't allow prisoners on that floor to smoke or talk. It was a place to cool down, to reflect on why you were there, to reflect on where you were going in life. Food was brought up three times a day on a little elevator, what they called a dumb waiter, into an open area at the end of the tier. We'd be let out one at a time to get our trays, and then back we'd go into our holes like rabbits to eat. Once a day, the area where we got the food became our exercise yard. We'd walk around for an hour or so, then they'd herd us back to our cells. At night, we'd have foam mattresses to soften the planks and some blankets to throw over us. These were taken away from us each morning.

After a month of that, I was glad to get back to William Head. It was almost Christmas. The sky was grey and the leaves were gone from the trees. The place looked barren, dismal, cold and empty. Lifeless. I got my old job back—carving. But the guys in the art shop, they were mostly whites who didn't like natives, so I took my soapstone and gear and went away from there. I carved down at the point, down at the beach where I could be by myself, with only the odd squirrel dashing around to keep me company as the waves crashed against the shore. I'd stay down there all day and sometimes into the evening, all by myself, sitting down carving on the edge of the ocean. I'd look up at the sky and I could see all the stars I used to travel by with the dog teams in winter up in the North. I wished I was there then, as I do now. Instead, I was a prisoner. They locked my body up and locked up my mind, too. I was getting headaches and sometimes I couldn't see properly. My memory was going. Too much tension. My insides were gnawing again. I had to get out of there, to be free to roam again.

Christmas came and about a hundred inmates were sent out on passes to spend Christ's birthday with their families. I couldn't be sent anywhere. The North Pole was too far away for me to get to in a couple of days. So I was left behind. I had a pretty good time anyway. Somebody slipped me some booze and it relaxed my mind for a little while.

Six months later, I got a one-day pass. Not a real pass. Just sort of an okay to go to town for the afternoon to see a halfway house that was being opened as part of the rehabilitation program for natives.

I thought that while I was out I might as well look up one of the girls I'd met in camp. I looked for her in a hotel bar. She wasn't there. But I thought since *I* was there, I might just as well sit down and have a drink. I did. The drink turned into two, three, six, seven. Before I knew it my head was spinning and I felt as free as a caribou roaming the slopes of the Richardson Mountains. I left that bar and headed down the street. I was my old self again. Just a few more drinks, I thought, then I'd head back to serve my time behind that skinny wire fence.

Late that afternoon, I could hardly see for the alcohol coursing through my veins. I was swaggering, on top of the world, waving at passers-by on the main street of Victoria, shouting hellos to hookers. I had to take a pee. Well, no place like the gutter. Used to do it all the time in Inuvik.

I was looking down, intent on the little stream flowing down off the curb into the street when I heard a car screeching to a stop a few feet away.

"Got a pretty full bladder there, partner!"

Wheeling around, I tripped on my pants, falling on my bare ass. It was a policeman.

"Better come along with me," he said.

Like hell, I thought. I swung my arm and grabbed his leg, trying to pull him down. It was a stupid thing to do. There were two of them and they pinned my head to the pavement with no effort at all. A crowd gathered as I screamed and shouted. Soon a paddy wagon arrived and I struggled and fought with them as they forced me into it.

I spent the night in police custody and the next morning I was on my way back to the B.C. Pen's special detention wing.

You're not supposed to speak in those little cubbyholes, so I laughed. I laughed, even though I was sick and hungry. I did it just to keep those guards on edge. I laughed for fifteen days. Didn't eat a thing. Didn't want their slop. I threw it back at them. Refused the water, too. And there was shit and piss all over my cell. I didn't care.

I'd given up caring. I wasn't going to get out of there anyway. I was a prisoner of the white man for life. I knew it. I knew it then. I was finished. My head hurt and my memory was full of holes, like a sieve. I was slowly going out of my mind.

* * * * * *

In early September of 1972 I was taken to the office of the prison psychiatrist and given some paper on which I wrote down my thoughts about the prison system, about my life in the North and on Skid Row. Then they took me to the doctor. He told me there was a place, a hospital in the Fraser Valley that was like a prison, a maximum-security prison, but where they looked after you when your head is sick. I knew mine was.

I stood before him, my body reeking with urine. I hadn't washed nor shaved in the month since I'd arrived.

"Put me in," I pleaded. "Put me in that place. I need that kind of treatment. I couldn't get it at P.A., or William Head, or the B.C.P., or any of those institutions I'd been in before."

I could hardly hold back the tears. I was desperate for treatment, anything that would slow my spinning head, set it straight for once and for all. There was a slim chance they could fix it, and I could live in happiness, free again. I hoped they could.

"Okay, Tony," he nodded. "Now take it easy. Everything will be fine. You'll hear from us in a few days."

I was released to the population at the B.C.P., put in "A" cellblock in the very bottom of the penitentiary. The plaster was cracking, caving in. There were writings scrawled on the walls, some of them put there years before by inmates probably long dead. There were holes near the floor and I could see rats and mice scurrying in and out of them. Garbage was strewn throughout the place and everywhere there was the stink—like I don't know what—of piss and shit and sweaty armpits. My cell was covered with dirt that I guess had been piling up ever since they opened that pen way back in the last century. I thought they had put me in an old mine shaft it was so dark and dirty.

Almost every guy in there was waiting to be sent to that hospital in the Fraser Valley. There were fights every day. Real crazy nuts mixing it up. I tried to stay out of their way. They didn't bother me much anyway. A lot of them were Indians I knew from the street and from Prince Albert.

Right next to me was a queer guy. He was in for rape. I was sitting in my cell with the door open when a fella named Price, a real wicked one, went by the front of my cell. He had a strange mischievous look on his face and I went out to see what he was up to.

Price shuffled down the landing to the end of the cells to a water tap we used for filling our wash basins. He turned on the tap, and let it run till the water was real hot, boiling. Then he picked up a bucket of scalding water. He ran past me to that queer guy standing at the front of his cell. And Price let him have it. He splashed the water all over that skinner. He was screaming, burning with hot water. Hollering for his life in there. And Price, I could see him running down past the cells on the other side with the empty pail. He was laughing. I could see his mouth wide open and his eyes dancing with insane delight. But I couldn't hear his laughter. It was drowned out by the skinner's cries for help. He was in the back of his cell now, squirming under his blankets, trying to ease the pain on his face and chest and legs. The guards came running and they moved him up to a special segregation cell. Protective custody. They had to do that. Someone would eventually have killed him.

His cell was taken up by a young kid, no more than

sixteen or seventeen. I thought, what the hell, maybe he's okay, and I walked over and said hello. He seemed all right, and we talked for a while. As I was leaving, the kid said I should come back and see him at nine o'clock, just before bedtime. I thought nothing of it. I had supper and read a bit. And when nine o'clock rolled around, I strolled out of my cell to see what the kid wanted.

The silly bugger. I couldn't believe my eyes. He was standing in the shadows at the rear of his cell, with his back to me. He had nothing on but a pair of ladies' panties. His shoulder length hair and smooth skin—it made him look like—you know that magazine, *Playboy*? . . . it made him look like one of the girls in the centrefold.

"How do I look?" he said.

"You look okay."

I smiled and tried to make believe I didn't know what he was trying to show me. I walked back to my cell and lay there looking at the ceiling for a long time. I hardly heard the crash of the cell doors being locked that night. I was on my way to a hospital for the criminally insane, not any better, I guessed, than that sick queer in the cell next to me, no better than Price the sadist. I only hoped that hospital could do something to help.

19

Silent Too Long

Eskimo mythology tells of the time when . . .

The first of my people came on the ice, blown by the wind, brought by the magic of the Northern Lights and the North Wind. These people became great hunters. They used to hunt the cave bear that was as big as a whale-boat. The bear's tracks were so big a man could kneel in them. In those days the sea otter and the sea mink were bigger than man. The mink would chase boats and wait for men to fall overboard. They were man-eaters. In those days, in the Smoky Mountains were small people, about one foot tall. The children of these people used one caribou ear for a parka. They lived in trees and in houses built in the ground.

And every time the half moon tipped, game was plenty.

Then something called the new life came. The white man came from the outside world. My people were good hunters. My people were good trappers. My people were good fishermen. Now they are dying. The Inuit are dying. I can hear the story in the wind, which has come to take us away . . .

The land that was great has little game. The land of the caribou cannot feed my family. The musk ox, our pride, has almost gone. The white fox is nearly gone from the ice. The Great Nanook is nearly gone from the ice. The seal for my kayak has nearly gone from the sea. The walrus for my meal is nearly gone from the sea. The white whale that brought my muktuk is going away. The black whale is going too. The fast-flying Atput duck is leaving. The King Loon is going away, and the King Eider Duck. The salmon is leaving the river, and the Arctic char is going away, with the white fish and the herring.

I can see all these things going away forever from the land. The beautiful narwhal is going too. I can see the Northern Lights. In the cold nights the full moon still shines, the night owl still calls. My family is awake and cannot sleep. The wolf calls to the full moon, but my dogs, the huskies, don't answer the wolf call. Listen to the North Wind. It has come to take us away. The name, Inuvialuit, will only be heard in the wind. The land will still be there, the moon will still shine, the Northern Lights will still be bright, and the Midnight Sun will still be seen. But we will be gone forever . . .

* * * * *

We can never go back.

We, the Eskimo people are like the sun spots which sometimes appear on the lens of an astronomer. We are in the way, we blur the picture the white man has of the future of the North.

I see us starving while others get rich from the oil and mineral resources, crushed by the emerging giant like a page out of Eskimo mythology.

We are people who keep everything locked up inside our minds. We have been afraid of insulting the white man. Now, when we need his help, he doesn't understand us.

So a race of proud, silent people will die . . . my brothers and sisters . . . too humble and confused to complain, to cry out.

I have pains in my head from Skid Row beatings and too much drink and my stomach hurts from the wrong kind of food.

It's funny, but I can't get angry, even though they put me in a cage. Eskimos don't get angry over something they can't control or understand.

I remember once, some whales were trapped in the Husky Lakes. We wanted to kill them instead of watching them starve. We knew they would die for sure. But the white man's law had come and it wouldn't allow us to do what our senses told us to do. We could have made use of the whales for food, but we could only stand there and watch helplessly for many days until they starved to death. It was a slow, useless death.

At Paulatuk the seal hunting was good. We got a lot of meat and a fair price for the skins. Then, suddenly, the top price for a sealskin dropped to eight dollars. The white man had learned of the value of sealskin and had come in to hunt them. Following that there were the newspaper stories about the clubbing of defenceless baby seals. As a result we heard that a ban on seal hunting was coming. The Eskimo had never clubbed seals, but the ban applied to us as well as the white man. That year we nearly starved, living on a little tom cod fish and not much else. We could not raise enough money to buy ammunition for hunting caribou. We barely made it through the winter.

It is a story of misunderstanding repeated many times from the first time the white man set foot in the North.

A group of early explorers who crossed the Arctic returned home claiming that the Eskimo regarded the white man as an inferior. To support this they quoted the Eskimo word "inuvialuit"—the name we use for our people, meaning "the real man". It does not mean that we think we are superior. It is simply used as an expression to describe the whole Eskimo family as one ... man, woman and child.

The culture gap, which divides our community from the people in the South, has constantly been underestimated.

The tax system was applied to us when we didn't know what taxes were. When we received the first income tax forms we thought someone was trying to sell us something and we used them to light the stoves. Once, I simply signed my name on the form and mailed it back to the capital of Canada in Ottawa with a note saying I didn't know how to fill it out. They mailed it right back with a note from a computer saying, "Fill out the form properly." T4 slips were so baffling to Eskimos that many either threw them away or kept them as souvenirs. What is an Eskimo supposed to do with sheets of paper with hundreds of numbers on them?

The government civil servants, sent to the North to help us with our problems, collected their pay and did nothing. They might ask a question or two twice a year, but they knew nothing of the day-to-day living of the Eskimo. I know of only one civil servant who ever entered an Eskimo house to ask about our problems.

The church is the same. The church has been selling tickets to heaven for years, but none of the money has ever gone back to help the Eskimo. It has a strong hold over us still. The church says give and you shall receive ... yet it collects and goes on taking.

My father gave his life to the church, but it wasn't enough. When he was helpless and no longer able to work for the missionaries, the church abandoned him.

When the white man came North in the fifties he brought knives and forks with him. It was a small thing but it should have been a warning because you could see the Eskimo children growing away from their parents even then. The young Eskimos would use the knives and forks to cut and eat raw frozen meat, while their elders sat beside them holding their meat in their hands and chewing on it in the traditional way.

From too many years in school, Eskimo children have even forgotten how to speak our language. When they come home they can't communicate with their parents. They are not thinking the same thoughts, or speaking the same words.

Listen . . .

The sound of the wind is disturbed with noise. I awake while the moon is still awake. I look out of my igloo to see Nanook eating. He is eating my seal blubber, but I let him go. The dogs are noisy, but then still. I have caribou meat for my family to eat. In a stone pot, I make some broth. We have our morning meal . . . the hot broth and frozen meat.

My woman, Oomaga, looks at my torn shoes. She picks up her bone needle and caribou sinew. The stitches she sews I can hardly see . . . they are so small. My son will be a great hunter some day soon. My daughter will be a sewing woman soon.

I fix the sinew string on my caribou horn bow. I fix my arrows with caribou bone heads. I fix my harpoon with walrus head, tusk and hide. My sled is made of wood, tied with sealskin thong. My sled runners are made of whale rib bone. My dogs' harnesses are made of seal hide. The dogs' collars are from caribou hide. I have to go hunting for meat from Tuktu, the caribou. Kibmitka, my dogs, are ready with the sled.

I pick up my harpoon, my bow and arrows, and some frozen meat. I also take some seal blubber for my dogs to eat. I put on my hunting shoes, the soles have three inches of fur. They will kill any sound I make that the wind can't drown. I take my family with me, wrapped up in the sled, wrapped in warm caribou and polar bear hides. I leave my empty igloo behind.

My dogs smell something, something in the wind, out on

the sea ice. I let them go. They lead us to the ice, and I see the seal holes. I let my dogs loose to find some more of them. I crouch beside one of the breathing holes, and wait. I take my harpoon, and wait for the seal, over his hole. He comes up for air. I wait till he stops bobbing in the water and takes a breath. I get him.

My woman skins the seal, and cuts the meat. We gather and eat the meat and blubber while it is still warm. I build our new igloo with my bone snowknife. When I finish my igloo, my woman brings the hides. The floor is caribou and polar bear skins. Our mattress is musk ox hide and caribou hide. My family dresses in caribou skins and the lamp, which is also a stove, is a big dishlike soap stone which holds seal oil for fuel. The wick is moss. The fire is made with a bow stick bit, which is a kind of hand drill. I insert it in a hole filled with dry cotton wood. Friction from the spinning stick causes a spark. Wild cotton-like flax that grows in the Arctic tundra I put on the spark, and I nurse it with my breath until it catches fire. I put small shavings on the cotton, and I blow some more to build the flames.

I feed my dogs seal blubber, then leave the seal fat a distance from my igloo. Nanook, the polar bear, will sniff it out. In the moonlight, I will get Nanook by this bait. I wait with my harpoon, my knife, my bow and arrow. Kibmitka, my dogs, will tell me when Nanook comes. Nanook is strong and dangerous.

This night, the Northern Lights come out to help me see. The great Nanook comes to eat my seal blubber bait. I take my harpoon with the long walrus tusk spearhead. I turn my dogs loose. They chase Nanook. The dogs nip and surround him. My aim is true with the harpoon, and Nanook dies. We have meat of the great Nanook to eat. We have his thick, warm fur to keep us warm. The dogs eat, and they are happy and play in the snow.

This night, we thank the Medicine Man. He can hear us and see us from far away. After our meal of seal meat,

Nanook meat, and broth, I tell my family a story of my Atatak, my grandfather. It is time for my family to sleep. They turn inside out their shoes, mitts, trousers and parkas to dry the skins. They curl up in one bed against the cold, naked. Their bodies and the fur hides keep them warm. I stay up and listen to the North Wind howl, the ice crack.

If the wind changes direction, the sea may take us away, to be lost forever. But the North Wind stays, and my family sleeps. The dogs hear the lone wolf howl inland, and answer the call. I care about tonight . . . tomorrow is another day. Finally I, too, fall asleep. I dream of great days of hunting to come.

When I awake, the northeast wind is strong and cold, and we move to Nunna, the land. I make a new igloo, and my woman fixes the inside with fur. I move just in time, for the wind takes the ice away. The spirit of the wind gave me the warning to move. Now the wind blows strong, the storm is blinding. My dogs, though, go to sleep.

Here in the igloo, my children want to hear Unipkarq, a story. I pick up my Krilaun, Eskimo drum. I sing of how I make my kayak, my canoe. I sing of how I make my Angooni, my paddle. I sing of how I will paddle my kayak. I sing of my uncle, who will help me paddle. I sing of the seal hunt with my uncle years ago. Now he is gone, like the wind, and I am alone.

My woman tells me it is time to sleep. The children are asleep already, and they dream of my songs and my stories. Now in the wind I hear a faint call. The wise old wolf is calling his kind to hunt. The storm is his screen. When the hunt is good, his call is silence. I fix the seal oil lamp, then sleep, dreaming of the wild caribou herds, and the great musk ox hunts of my people.

Now our young people are put in schools to learn the white man's language and customs while our culture dies. I don't think there is one young Eskimo in school today who can tell a story and act it out at the same time, or complete a carving which tells a story out of the Eskimo past.

I once asked an Eskimo boy of sixteen, who came to me for food, "Why don't you come hunting with me, so you can get some fur for clothes, and seal meat to eat?"

His answer: "I don't know how to shoot or hunt and I don't want to get bloody or dirty."

I told him: "You don't have to shoot and hunt. I'll do that and you can just watch and help a little."

Said the boy: "I don't want anything to do with hunting and shooting. Only savages do that."

But there were no jobs in the South for him. And with none of the old skills behind him he was forced to drift into welfare . . . part of the lost race.

I have watched these boys go out to look for work when there were no permanent jobs to be found, only summer work handling freight and deckhand jobs on ships. In the winter these boys, who should have known how to trap and hunt, to support their families, had to rely on their parents for food and shelter. When their parents can no longer support them, welfare is there . . .

I remember a politician coming to our village many years ago promising welfare for everyone if we voted for him. The Eskimos asked me: "What is welfare?"

Now there is no need to ask. Welfare is everywhere in the North, like the snow in winter.

Thirty dollars they used to get, those single Eskimos who couldn't hunt or fish or find jobs . . . thirty dollars to last thirty-one days in temperatures of sixty and seventy below zero.

A widow with eight children got one hundred dollars a month. I saw large families get sick and starve.

Giving the Eskimo welfare is like giving a hard-working engine too little oil. After a while it burns itself out and doesn't work any more.

They tell us to get jobs, yet there are few jobs.

When we do get hired, it is often for not longer than two months and twenty-nine days. We are laid off then because, after three months, we would have to be regarded as permanent workers entitled to benefits like northern allowance and isolation pay.

We pay unemployment insurance, but we never get to collect it because we don't keep the jobs long enough to qualify. And we pay into the social security scheme even though few Eskimos live to be 65 years old.

When we are laid off we have nothing to do but drift to Inuvik, to that part of the town, the west end, that is like a Skid Row transported from the South. Teepee Town. In 1963 I was beaten up there and left in the snow to bleed to death in forty-below weather. I made it to the police station to lay a complaint and they locked me up, then fined me for being drunk in a public place.

My people have been sent to jail for no reason except that they did not understand the words used in court by lawyers and prosecutors. We have accepted justice while not understanding it. Eskimos don't win court cases. How can they, when they don't know what the word "guilty" means?

I didn't understand when they told me to swear on the Bible. I didn't know what they meant by "testimony" when I was put on the witness stand.

But it isn't only the words, it's our philosophy. We don't fight for our rights because we are a docile people, trusting and loving.

One Eskimo I knew got a job on the DEW Line. He didn't like the job and he just wanted to hunt and trap again, but he didn't know how to quit. He said, "Maybe I'll get lucky and be fired sometime. Then my family can eat good meat again."

My story is a little like that . . . about a man, an innocent, who tried to join the march of civilization without knowing of the dangers that could trip and squash him.

Of the thirty Eskimos I knew well on the course that first brought me South, seven were dead and seventeen were either sick or jobless by the time I went to jail in Calgary. I learned this in a letter from home. It seems as if the people in the South help those in need in foreign countries but forget about their own people in the North.

I hear on the radio that the United States and Canada are squabbling over who has sovereignty in Arctic waters. What they are talking about is my people's hunting grounds. We were hunting on the Arctic Ocean before the white man came to discover America. I hope they leave us a little salt water.

Instead of fighting for our land we welcomed the white man right into our igloos. But there are no princes or princesses in our legends, so to him we are savages and he hunts down our women for pleasure.

The Eskimo girl is lured by the white skin and blue eyes and the blonde hair. Then her white man returns to the South and she is left with a white baby. When fatherless children are left behind, they grow up on welfare, or are cared for by Eskimos who are too humble to complain. Two of my sisters have illegitimate children by white men who have disappeared, so I have cute little blue-eyed nephews and nieces. We don't discriminate against these children. We give them the family name. They will grow up, with our own children, ashamed to admit they are Eskimo.

They will learn to build capital, learn that it is good to possess more than your next-door neighbour. There used to be no such thing as theft in an Eskimo community. We would use what we needed and return it when we were finished. Selfishness was looked upon as foolishness. A man who was afraid to share with his neighbour was a lonely man. Our doors used to be open to all. Now we lock our doors, we are afraid of other human beings.

Soon we will be afraid to welcome even our own relations.

In Edmonton I saw white people walk by an Indian girl—some were even smiling—as she hemorrhaged in the street. Maybe I should have laughed too, left her there to bleed, but I was brought up in the old way. I pulled Fred Wolkie out of ice water at Aklavik, saved George Banikland from choking on a spoon, pulled George Tardiff out of the water when he fell off a barge, saved the life of a boy, Jonah Nakimayak, when he was threatened by a rabid dog at Cape Parry, transported Eric Lester thirty miles by dog team when he was unconscious with a leg wound, carried Walter Bennett home when he shot himself in the foot, took Eva Panaktak to a nurse so she could have her baby . . . I could go on and on. I risked my life to save the lives of at least five people, and helped many others to survive hunger and cold. Like any Eskimo I have a natural instinct to help anyone in trouble, but when I watched the white people walk past the Indian girl I wondered how long it would take until we were the same. I was frightened.

In 1957 there was a tent pitched next to the DEW Line. I went in and saw an Eskimo woman sick with the 'flu and measles, which is a killer-disease to the Eskimo. Her four children had measles also. Her husband was sick, too, but still he looked for food . . . in the garbage dump.

"Who brought this disease called measles?" I thought. It was not here before the white man came. Neither was the garbage dump. And I cried for the Eskimo, and his family, and for all Eskimos.

The DEW Line? A series of stations across the Arctic to warn the U.S. and Canada of attack. But the Eskimo does not need the DEW Line. Who would want to attack us? We know there are Russians but we have no need to fear them. And we like the Japanese. They are friendly people. The communist Chinese have a culture that is quite similar to ours. We both believe in equality for everybody. The community works together and shares. No one capitalizes in any way and no one tribe dominates another. So the early warning system is for people in the South, not for us. No one would ever drop a bomb on the Eskimos. Only greedy, proud and selfish people fight.

No, we do not need the DEW Line, yet it has spoiled trapping. Garbage from the stations is thrown into the sea and refuse can be found all over the Arctic coast.

Oil explorations have resulted in the deaths of thousands of fish which were left to drift down the Mackenzie River. These same explorations have destroyed thousands of miles of timber in trapping country. The ships that will carry oil in the Arctic will destroy our trapping and hunting on the ice. Water and air pollution will eventually destroy the foxes, seals and polar bears. The fish and the whales will be gone from the Arctic Ocean. Finally the Eskimos will be gone.

I say for the last time. We have been silent too long.